Drops
of
Rain

BEVERLY FONTENOT

COVER DESIGN BY
DAVID SILVER

ISBN 978-1-64028-409-8 (paperback)
ISBN 978-1-64028-410-4 (digital)

Christian Faith Publishing, Inc.
832 Park Avenue
Meadville, PA 16335
www.christianfaithpublishing.com

Printed in the United States of America

DEDICATION

To all those who need a drop of rain to clarify the message of the Father, Son, and Holy Spirit beyond their own understanding and to help them along their journey, *Drops of Rain* and its companion, "Chewing on the Word," is dedicated.

Sometimes, Christians need to be reminded that faith relies on the spiritual, the unseen, rather than the seen. This is like the faith from which Christianity sprung or from the faith of Abraham, Isaac, and Jacob. Consider the following statement which comes from a website titled "Ancient Jewish History: The Ark of the Covenant." It states, "Jews had no physical manifestation of God on earth. As a rule, Judaism rejects spiritual manifestations of spiritually preferring instead to focus on actions and beliefs. Christianity believes Jesus is not just a prophet or a teacher, but he is God himself. He is threefold, the Father, Son, the Holy Spirit."

Kenneth Haggin wrote in his book, *Health Food Devotions*, what it means to have faith. He said, "It means to call those things that be not as though they were."

CONTENTS

TITLES RELATED TO THEMES

Title and Number	Themes
Forgiveness and Calvary, 1	Forgiveness
Satan Cannot Read Our Thoughts, 2	Satan Cannot Read Thoughts
Grief, 3	Forgiveness
Obedience, 4	Obedience
Obedience: the Served Is the Servant, 5	Obedience
Love, 6	Love
Love, Again, 7	Love
Pride, Love, 8	Love
Fear, 9	Fear
Perseverance, 10	Patience, Perseverance
Choice, 11	Choice
Love Over Hate, 12	Love
Faith (a, b, c), 13	Faith
Mercy, 14	Judgment
Backsliders, Backsliding, Redemption, 15	Redemption
Heavy Burden, 16	Patience, Perseverance
Afflict, 17	Afflict
Sowing and Reaping, 18	Sowing and Reaping
Mustard Seed Faith, 19	Faith
Good Courage Isn't Fear, 20	Good Courage
God Inhabits Praise, 21	Good Courage
Wasn't Adam the Son of God Too, 22	Not a Proselyte
Sin ~ Transgression ~ Breaking the Law, 23	Transgression

PREFACE

"Behold, the days come, saith the Lord God, that I will send a famine in the land, not a famine of bread, nor a thirst for water, but of hearing the words of the Lord: and they shall wander from sea to sea, and from the north even to the east, they shall run to and fro to seek the word of the Lord, and shall not find it," (Amos 8:11-12).

According to Scripture, those who will not thirst during those days shall be those who draw out their soul to the hungry, the homeless, the naked, family members. "And the Lord shall guide thee continually, and satisfy thy soul in drought, and make fat thy bones: and thou shalt be like a watered garden, and like a spring of water, whose waters fail not," (Isa. 58:11).

"But be ye doers of the word, and not hearers only, deceiving your own selves," (James 1:22).

ACKNOWLEDGEMENT

Praise and thanksgiving I give to Elohim for having brought about ~ revealed himself in *Drops of Rain's* companion book called Chewing on the Word. The following persons have been important to me in affirming my need to finish both *Drops of Rain*:

- my courageous daughter who puts others first.
- my wise and understanding grandson.
- my faithful and preserving granddaughter.
- my loving sister.
- my encouraging friend, Mary.
- my confirming pastor.

Concerning the last person credited, my pastor, he was sent by the C.M.E. (Christian Methodist Episcopal) church to pastor the church I attended. My membership at this church had started, I suppose, practically at my birth. Although he was not its pastor then, but he had become its pastor at a much later age of my life. Eventually, his ministry was relocated to a different church in a different city, but he continued his friendship with me and my family. One day he telephoned me, as he often did, but this time, not necessarily to ask about my welfare but to ask me if I knew anything about the book of Revelation. He had come, I knew, to respect my knowledge as a seminarian. I had attended Iliff School of Theology in Denver, Colorado, a United Methodist seminary. Almost before I could even hardly respond to his salutation, he asked, "Do you know anything about Revelation?" I almost fainted!

I had been wondering how Elohim would confirm this project, which included "Chewing on the Word" and now, the confirmation about the legitimacy of this project, which I titled Chewing on the Word, an integral part of *Drops of Rain*. I stuttered and answered, "Yes, I do. I just, almost simultaneously with your call, finished a first draft about the book of Revelation. It is an insight which God has given me. Would you like a copy?"

"Yes," responded the booming voice on the other end of the phone. I was ecstatic! I could not believe that this knowledgeable theologian would want to chew on this drop of rain. After he had received "Chewing on the Word," he responded without hesitation and affirmatively. His affirmation eased my doubts about "Chewing on the Word's" need to be shared.

INTRODUCTION

My thoughts about God the Savior, or Elohim, which have helped me become more aware are what I call drops of rain. The "rain" started years ago and continues. They do clarify Elohim's Word for me, and hopefully, they'll inspire and clarify his Word for others. These drops of rain have a twofold title which are *Drops of Rain* and Chewing on the Word.

Each part has its own significance. *Drops of Rain* magnifies Elohim's precepts, and "Chewing on the Word" sequences the book of Revelation. Some drops of rain have been written as they were received—in first person. Others have not been written in first person but have been written in second person and sometimes, third person.

MEMO

TO :
FROM :
RE :
DATE :

_____

1

FORGIVENESS AND CALVARY

Forgiveness is the past. Repentance is the present, alongside the future. Repentance was enacted by Jesus at Calvary. There, at Calvary, his Father forgave us for our transgression. He forgave what was owed him as a consequence of humanity's transgression. Consequently, humanity's transgression continues to be forgiven. This forgiveness was enacted by Elohim's Divine Son, Jesus, at the cross. Through his death, humanity can confess repentance and have the opportunity to receive eternal life. Before Jesus, there was John the Baptist with cries of repentance. John the Baptist cries, in verses 2 and 8 in Matthew chapter 3, "And saying, Repent ye: for the kingdom of heaven is at hand …. Bring forth therefore fruits meet for repentance."

Therefore, while John the Baptist came to baptize with water unto repentance, Jesus came to baptize with the Holy Ghost, or Holy Spirit, and with fire. Matthew 3:11 states, "I indeed baptize you with water unto repentance: but He that cometh after me is mightier than I, whose shoes I am not able to bear: he shall baptize you with the Holy Ghost, and with fire."

Jesus, before the repayment of humanity's debt to Elohim, by giving himself for us to God, was, and is, and will be, the personification of forgiveness.

Because of his debt to Elohim via himself, humanity is no longer unforgiven by God. God no longer remembers our sins. We have been forgiven! *Forgiveness is the past*. It's been done by Jesus. It is Calvary. All we have to do is receive it, and repent from daily sin. Repenting requires expressing being sorry for sins one has committed, alongside confessing them and not returning to those sins. The purpose of repenting is to change. Therefore, it feels as though forgiveness represents the past while repentance expresses present time. Followers of Jesus should strive to experience change akin to the transfiguration of Jesus.

2

SATAN CANNOT READ OUR THOUGHTS

This truth has been revealed: Satan cannot read our thoughts. He can only put thoughts into our mind, which he wants us to act on, so that they will cause damage or loosen our grip on the truth, and is where our power and strength derive.

This drop of rain was received by one other than myself. However, I have received similar drops of rain. Drop of rain 35 and drop of rain 104 appear similar to this drop of rain. These drops of rain are warnings. Warnings for humanity to not act upon evil thoughts. To be acted upon means they have to be spoken. Any thought lies dormant until it is spoken, or an unborn thought is one which is not spoken. To be spoken, the tongue must be used to speak the thought, to form words into a language which imitates the thought.

Spoken thoughts are placed into the heart, and they can condemn the speaker; or they can save, lift, or resurrect the speaker. Michal's thoughts condemned her when she used her tongue to create words about David. With her words, she tried to damage David's spirit to take away David's love for Elohim; but she failed, because it was her spirit which was damaged and not David's. David stood steadfast and patiently in his love for Elohim.

According to Webster's New World Dictionary, "damage" is defined as the hurting or the breaking of a thing so as to make it less valuable. Was this Michal's intent when she spoke harsh words to David about David's dancing before the Lord to show Elohim his adoration? Was David's heart broken by the thoughts Michal spoke, or was it her heart which was broken by the thoughts she spoke? Apparently, it was hers because her words brought about a consequence—the consequence of being childless until the day of her death. The episode between her and David appears in 2 Samuel 6, verses 14, 16, and 20. They are as follows: "And David danced before the Lord with all his might; and David was girded with a linen ephod," (v.14). "And as the ark of the Lord came into the city of David, Michal Saul's daughter looked through a window, and saw king David leaping and dancing before the Lord; and she despised him in her heart," (v.16). "Then David returned to bless his household. And Michal the daughter of Saul came out to meet David, and said, How glorious was the king of Israel to day, who uncovered himself to day in the eyes of the handmaids of his servants, as one of the vain fellows shamelessly uncovereth himself!" (v.20)

3

GRIEF AND FORGIVENESS

A few months ago, being somewhat aware of my feeling of anger, a small inward voice whispered, "You're grieving." "Grieving?" I questioned. I thought, "About what!" Nobody I knew had died recently. However, I quickly made a mental survey to make sure I had not thought incorrectly. "No," I had thought correctly; no one close to me had recently died. So why was I grieving? "Could grief and anger be the same?" I questioned myself. Since I did not know, I decided to consult the meaning of anger. I googled it.

What came up surprised me. Yes, anger and grief were the same. There stood grief as a synonym for anger; the two words were presented as one in the definition I had googled. So, I thought, "If both words were the same, what or whom had I not forgiven since anger is the by-product of not forgiving?" I knew, from my faith, that forgiveness is critical for one's wellness too spare! Therefore, why was I angry? If anger is as grief, and grief is brought about by a loss, then what loss or losses had I recently endured or suffered in order to experience anger brought on by grief or grief brought on by anger? Additionally, who or whom had I not forgiven? If to be angry is to not be forgiving, and if anger is as grief and if grief is as a loss, I wondered, "What had I lost?" I searched my mind for the things I had lost and was angry or unforgiving because of their loss, either consciously or unconsciously. Surely, there had been much, or many, things I had tried to hide or tuck away "beneath" the surface of my mind or into my subconscious. I recognized them now.

As I drew them close to the surface, I asked my Father, in the name of his Divine Son Jesus, to forgive me for these things while simultaneously knowing that this had been his Son's purpose on earth—to bring forgiveness to me for having done those sins. My faith told me that I would experience being delivered, freed, and saved with this forgiveness.

4

OBEDIENCE

Bringing my body into agreement, alignment, obedience, submission with God's Will is healing. We are to be aware that God's Will be done on earth; the same as it is done in heaven (Matt. 6:10). According to the words Jesus spoke, I as a believer that Jesus is the divine and only Son of Elohim. God can do the same works as the works He does, in addition to doing even greater works (John 14:13-14). Jesus complements his Father in John 14:13-14 when he states, "Whatever you or I ask God, in his name, he will do, so that the Father should be glorified." Therefore, I should be able to ask God confidently for things, in the name of Jesus, and God will hear my confident petition, on behalf of his Son Jesus. Honoring my request on behalf of Jesus honors and glorifies God. Remember, when we petition Elohim, we must have no hatred or be unforgiving in our heart toward others. First John 4:20-21 tells us this: "If a man say I love God and hate his brother, he is also a liar; for he that loves not his brother, whom he has seen, how can he love God whom he has not seen? And this commandment have we from him, that he who loves his brother loves God also."

5

OBEDIENCE. THE SERVED IS THE SERVANT AND THE SERVANT IS THE SERVED

Being a child of God is a reciprocal arrangement. I serve God ~ am obedient to God and God serves me ~ is faithful to me. God is in me, and I am in God. This drop of rain can be found in 1 John 4:13-21. Hence, a new approach might be taken in questioning. Questions about one's perfections, instead of inquisitions about one's imperfections, should perhaps be posed. This might be a good approach to be taken when one observes what it means for God to be in one, as one is in God. It becomes a reciprocal arrangement. Both Jesus and others are to be served as well as to serve. Reciprocity is an agreement entered into between servant and Master.

First John 4:13-16 states, "Hereby know we that we dwell in him, and he in us, because he has given us of his Spirit. And we have seen and do testify that the Father sent the Son to be Savior of the world. Whosoever shall confess that Jesus is the Son of God, God dwells In him, and he in God. And we have known and believed the love that God has for us. God is love; and he that dwells in love dwells in God, and God in him."

6

LOVE

According to 1 John 4:20, if one can't love one's neighbor whom one can see physically, how can one love Jesus whom one can't physically see? But in addition to love manifesting itself in loving one's neighbor, it manifests itself in long-suffering. Jesus Christ is patient, long-suffering, and/or persevering. The opposite of love is lust. Lust is short-lived. Lust is based on the eye, reason, and scientific evidence.

Love is a balm. Like an unseen suave which soothes the flesh as it inwardly erupts from the soul, the spiritual body, love does heal. Love says, "My brother and I are reciprocal." The head is not greater than the shoulder. Each part needs the other. No master is greater than the servant, and no servant is less than the master. The master and the servant reciprocate. Love is what the Father commands his creations to do. One should love one's brother and sister even without expecting one's love being returned.

7

LOVE, AGAIN

Take the self out of me, and let it just be love ~ loving others as thyself. Instead of just crediting thyself with one's own accomplishment, credit God too for having given you the ability for having created the accomplishment. Crediting God is one's awareness that he is inside one, and one is inside him. Together, we are in agreement; and with this agreement, all things are possible.

8

PRIDE, LOVE

Pride is unpleasant if it replaces the love of God for the love of self. Self is not greater than another, and another should not be valued greater than self. Hence, the master is not greater than the servant, nor the servant less than the master.

Everyone is equal according to Elohim. Elohim's commandment, "Love thy neighbor as one loves oneself," reflects this concept of equality and symbolizes the release of selfish pride.

9

FEAR

Who is God ~ Jesus? They, in One, are not fear when one is downgraded to having little food in one's house to feed one's family and/or others. They are not anxiety, uncertainty, and insecurity when the doctor gives one negative news about one's health or the health of a loved one. They, God and Jesus, are good courage.

Elohim is good courage too. Good courage is the opposite of fear—discouragement about a circumstance, situation.

Love is the opposite of fear. First John 4:18 states, "There is no fear in love; but perfect love casts out fear; because fear has torment. He that fears is not made perfect in love."

Elohim wants humanity to beware or be aware of the enemy because the enemy comes in like a flood. One drop of rain stated, "Yes, yes, yes, for the enemy, the enemy comes in once again like a flood; but, oh, beware, beware he's coming. He's coming from the right and the left, and the north and the south, and the front and the back; but, beware, beware the enemy comes in like a flood. You may not see, you may not know, you may not understand. Be aware, be aware, be aware."

Isaiah 59:19 tells us that when the enemy comes in like a flood, the Spirit of the Lord will lift up a standard to be our support, our protection, our defense against the enemy: "So shall they fear the name of the Lord from the west, and his glory from the rising of the sun. When the enemy shall come in like a flood, the Spirit of the Lord shall lift up a standard against him."

In the Old Testament, God is depicted going before Israel in battles in order to protect them and help them defeat the enemies. This should have reminded Israel to be of good courage, to love, rather than to fear ~ be discouraged about and during difficult situations, circumstances. Love and good courage are similar in that they bring about a "standing," or the ability to stand. To stand is to persevere. Isaiah 40:31 is a reminder about what rewards will be brought about when one waits, perseveres, stands: "But they that wait upon the Lord shall renew their strength; they shall mount up with wings as eagles; they shall run and not be weary; and they shall walk and not faint."

Referring to good courage, Psalm 3:24 states, "Be of good courage, and He shall strengthen your heart, all ye that hope in the Lord."

Regarding resolving fear, Psalm 27:14 says, "Wait on the Lord: be of good courage, and he shall strengthen your heart: wait, I say, on the Lord."

God is not lukewarm, double-minded, wishy-washy, half-warm/half-cold, or confused. God is steadfast. Therefore, he is love, not fear. Where there is good courage, there is love, light, and right. Where there is fear, there is anxiety, fearfulness, darkness, and wrong.

Good courage cannot exist, does not exist, won't exist, alongside fear! Love has been crafted, created by Elohim ~ God for his creations. Fear was crafted by God, too, but to be used against his enemy, Satan, and not his children. It is the enemy who takes what God intended to be used against the enemy, Satan, and uses it against God's children; that is, only, if God's children do allow the enemy to do so. When Elohim ~ God is in his children, and his children are in Elohim, to be deceived by the enemy is highly unlikely.

10

PERSEVERANCE

Lord, thanks for the gift of perseverance ~ patience, long-suffering. This gift is as your love in that it can bring about holiness ~ righteousness. *Where Love Is, God Is* is the title of a play written by Leo Tolstoy. The play states that for love not to be, God is not. Similarly, God's love is patience because where there is patience and perseverance, there is Elohim. The evidence for Elohim's love is patience, his perseverance, his long-suffering.

If there appears to be no love in the family, say, "There is love in the family!" According to Rev. E. Hagin, faith and perseverance are intrinsic. One is essential, or necessary, for the construction of the other. Rev. Hagin says that faith is, "When one calls things that be, as if these things be not, or to be not as they were."

11

CHOICE

You and I have to make choices deliberately, and with serious thought. In considering choices, ask God to control your thinking so you'll know you're making a choice of understanding. A choice of understanding is a choice which will not separate you from God or put you on a path different from the one God intends for you to remain in order for him to be glorified by you. When Solomon asked God for wisdom, he was granted love. When he asked for understanding, he was given the talent to choose wisely in critical and difficult situations. They are decisions which fulfilled God's Word for Solomon's life in order that God would be glorified by Solomon's right decisions, decisions which led to God and not away, or apart, from God. This is understanding, and it is the thing for which Solomon asked.

God requires that our responses be affirmative rather than lukewarm. That we should affirm with yes or no rather than somewhere in between. Is this a reference to choice? Sometimes, especially as teens and young adults, the flesh feels pricked and tormented by having to be wise and understand things. We are left feeling tormented, trying to force ourselves into doing the right thing.

Additionally, like teens and young adults, older adults are beset with emotional confusion, anxiety, in an attempt to understand the dilemma of passing through daylight to twilight, from complete independence to dependence. Let the young adult, alongside the senior adult, also remember that God's Word said, "Be anxious for nothing." Let the young adult, alongside the senior adult, remember what has been revealed: "Things are not always as they seem." Also, let the young adult and the senior adult recall that God is our support, our standard, not our parents, mates, or our children. Isaiah 59:19 states, "When the enemy shall come in like a flood, the Spirit of the Lord shall lift up a standard against him." When my mother was dying, God reminded me that he had been, is and would be, my support, and that my mother had not been my support. After having been given this drop of rain, I willingly released my mother to go home to be with her heavenly Father.

Choice! What choice do I have? One choice ~ path leads solely to the satisfaction of the flesh with no thought about the lives of others. This path is a selfish path. Remember pride is only pride when it excludes the real purpose of life—helping others. Also, remember, we can only love Jesus when we feed his sheep, which is also the same as letting our light shine so that others will see in us the Son of God, Jesus! Be patient when making choices. Take as much time as necessary, in order to try not to stumble from Elohim's path he chose for you. Remember, one's path leads to him and requires understanding while the other departs from him and lacks understanding. Pride is only pride when one loves self so much that one can't or wills not to love God first and consequently fails to feed God's sheep, which is to love others as one loves self, which is Elohim's first commandment.

12

LOVE OVER HATE

Father, let me choose love over hate. I desire to be aware that every time I choose to speak negative words for any reason about a thing, this is fear - hate not love. First John 4:20-21 states: "If a man says I love God, and hates his brother, he is also a liar; for he that loves his brother whom he has not seen, how can he love God whom he has not seen? And this commandment have we from him, that he who loves his brother loves God."

I need to say those things that be not, as though they were. This is faith, belief.

13 (a)

FAITH

Faith is God's testimony to himself. God being a witness to himself about my obedience to him. What pleases God is that when I've been tried and tested over and over again, I have patience, I persevere, I stand. The reason for God being able to testify upon himself, be a witness to himself, and I about things is because there is nothing higher than himself; and "himself" is God. The Alpha and the Omega is the truth! Realistically, I can't be a witness about self because self was not first, or I am not Alpha and Omega. Because I am neither, I possess not the truth. The truth existed prior to self. Myself is not the Word. God is the True Word. God is higher than I. However, in a court of human law, I am recognized as a witness. I become legally compelled to swear upon myself as truth. Strange? Yes, it is strange because as a child of Elohim, this is spiritually impossible. Why? Because God is First Fruit, not self. Being First Fruit, Elohim can confirm the truth of my word and his Word, not I.

My obedience to Elohim's Word and his confirming my obedience to his Word activates God's faith. His faith or belief in my righteousness ~ love for him. God is pleased by his children's obedience. God was pleased with Abel's obedience when Abel gave God the first and best parts from his labor. God was pleased with his Son, Jesus, when Jesus resisted temptation and acted with patience and· perseverance during his time of extreme trial and tribulation. Are obedience and perseverance rewarded? I believe they are. Enoch's obedience was rewarded because he experienced a "spiritual death" instead of a physical death. Noah persevered, and his family and livestock escaped the flood. The earth was repopulated because of Noah's obedience. It was his genealogy which produced Jesus the Messiah. The same Jesus who presently sits next to his Father, Elohim, in heaven as high priest since he rose from the dead. It is Jesus's obedience and faith in his Father which brings about victory for Elohim's children and victory for his children against his enemy.

How long is it necessary for one to have patience, to persevere, before one receives compensation for one's obedience to Elohim or for him to answer one's confident request which he hears? David, in Psalm 62, talks about waiting on the Lord: "Truly, my soul waits upon God: from him cometh my salvation. He only is my rock and my salvation; he only is my defense; I shall not be greatly moved ... My soul, wait thou upon God; for my expectation is from him. He only is my rock and my salvation: he is my defense; I shall not be moved."

13 (b)

FAITH

Faith is God's testimony to himself. God is a witness to himself about my obedience to him. What pleases God is that after being tried over and over, one remains patient and perseveres. Perseverance through patience is an act of love, and God is love. He is patience and does persevere. He is slow to judge one for one's actions. When Elohim does judge, He judges fairly. He judges fairly because he is, has been, and will be. He is Alpha and Omega. His being of Alpha and Omega brings about him being able to wait patiently on me to act according to his will, to align my will with his will. He knew me before I was born and planned who I should become, but he leaves it up to us to choose to follow the "right" path, to step correctly. God is the truth. He is not a pretender or a hypocrite. A hypocrite is a pretender because a pretender gives false information. False information is untrue information. To be a hypocrite is an act of transgression against Elohim. God ~ Elohim is not a hypocrite because his testimony is absolute and true.

God is love. Fear ~ anxiety does not exist within Elohim. Where there is anxiety, there is fear, because fear and anxiety are synonyms. Fear casts out love. Where there is love, there must not be any anxiety. Anxiety and confidence do not coexist. They are opposites. A lack of confidence is a lack of faith, belief, trust, hope, expectation. Love perseveres and is not impatient with things. David sings about perseverance in Psalms 62:1-2: "Truly, my soul waits upon God:

from him comes my salvation. He only is my rock and my salvation; he only is my defense; I shall not be greatly moved."

Isaiah 40:28-31 talks about patience, perseverance, waiting on the Lord: "But they that wait upon the Lord shall renew their strength; they shall mount up with wings as eagles; they shall run and not get weary: and they shall walk and not faint."

Isaiah 40:7-8 reminds us that the Spirit is everlasting. It does not fade or evaporate. The Spirit has the ability to stand, to not wither like grass. One's spirit belongs to Elohim. It witnesses, it testifies, it judges. It is faithful and a testimony to himself about himself. Isaiah 40:7-8 states, "The grass withereth, the flower fadeth: because The Spirit of the Lord bloweth upon it: Surely The people is grass. The grass withereth, the Flower fadeth: but the Word of our shall stand Forever."

13 (c)

FAITH

Seeing a phenomenon with the physical eye doesn't always make the condition true nor is it not necessarily evidence for the situation not existing—not being true, not being real. Faith does not require physical evidence; only science requires physical evidence. Faith is confidence, hope, trust, expectation in things. We tend to want God to always respond quickly to the things for which we ask or petition. We like to receive miraculously. However, this mostly is not the case although sometimes, it could be. God is the Creator, and he controls situations. To consider him not controlling the situation, because we cannot wait or are impatient for his answer, is untrue. God is patient, and he perseveres. His waiting does not make him less the truth or unhearing; it makes him the judge and gives him the right to decide when he will give a judgment or his answer. No, his waiting does not make him hard of hearing; and a drop of rain received confirmed this. This drop of rain said, "I get tired of hearing! So stand on the Word! This is your transgression. Look not at the circumstance but me, the Word."

John 5:14-15 says Elohim tells us the same thing. It says when we ask him in confidence, in faith he hears. It states, "And this is the confidence I have in him, that if I ask anything according to his will, he hears me. And if I know he hears whatever I ask, I know that I have the petitions that I desired of him."

14

MERCY

It is difficult to imagine how there is love where mercy is lacking or mercy where knowledge lacks. Is this the reason God instructed Job to forgive his friends for trying to be Elohim when they did not exist before Elohim? For trying to be judge or playing judge when Elohim is the judge? When one takes the place of God by trying to judge others, this is not pleasing to Elohim. Judging others is out of God's Will because it makes one appear as Elohim's equal. Judging others implies one is before God. To be ahead of Elohim is impossible since Elohim's creation superseded his creations. Judging others is a transgression which necessitates forgiveness. Thus, Elohim required Job to seek forgiveness for his judgmental friends and himself. How had Job acted against Elohim which necessitated his need to repent in order to bring about Elohim forgiving Job? Job's action was that he took his mind off Elohim and looked at his circumstance as a result of being judged by his friends. Job's friends had not shown love to Job because they had not shown mercy or kindness to Job. They turned him away from the Creator to focus his attention on his natural, physical situation rather than the spiritual situation of mercy and love. According to the *Merriam-Webster* dictionary, the synonyms for mercy are kindness and bless. It says about mercy the following, "Kindness is to a wrong doer or enemy that which is greater than might be expected. The power to forgive or be kind." Consequently, one can imagine that judging others is the opposite of being merciful or kind to others alongside love being the opposite of "judge."

Remember Jesus's response to Simeon Peter when Peter tried to judge how long John would live? He wanted to know if John, Jesus's beloved disciple, would live a long life. Since it was not Peter's business to judge, but Jesus's business to know how long John would live, Jesus told Peter not to judge. Jesus said, "If I will that he tarry till I come, what is that to you? Follow me." Thus, Jesus warns his followers to be concerned about following him, and he will judge. He will judge the righteous from the unrighteous. He will decipher right from the wrong. He will decide what should be and what should not be! Following Jesus compels us to show mercy and kindness to others and not judgment.

15

BACKSLIDERS, BACKSLIDING, REDEMPTION

When people first "get saved," it is thought that they have accepted God ~ Elohim as being the Father of his only begotten Divine Son, Jesus, and have accepted Jesus as the Messiah of the world who gave his life so that God would pardon the sins of his children. He makes them free to not spend eternity, after their physical life ends, in hell instead of spending it in heaven alongside God ~ Elohim. With the passage of time, some new believers may become negligent in reading the Word ~ the Holy Bible, of which there are presently many versions in addition to the original King James Version. The newness of the experience wanes, and the excitement wears off. Consequently, they may fail to study God's Word daily. However, the only way to find God is by studying his Word. God plays hide and seek. To find him, one must seek or study his Word. Studying God in a physical church building "religiously" each Sunday is done by many. Hearing the Word of God in a physical building has been useful to some. For example, if the slaves, who'd been forcibly removed from their ancestral homelands on the African continent, had been stopped from attending church services in a physical building where they'd been given access to the Bible, many would have never had the opportunity to read or know their Savior. Many would have never have had the opportunity to be redeemed.

16

HEAVY BURDEN

"Don't try to carry the burden all by yourself. It is too heavy! Let me help you carry it! Together we can carry it. Yoked, we can carry it! It is too heavy for you to carry it all by yourself. It is too heavy for you to carry it alone. Let me help you carry it, because it's light for me."

Matthew 11:28-30 says, "Come unto me, all ye that labor and are heavy laden, and I will give you rest. Take my yoke upon you and lean on me; for I am meek and lowly at heart: and you shall find rest unto your souls. For my yoke is easy, and my burden is light."

When we look into the dictionary, "meek" is given as an adjective and means, "patient and mild, not showing anger, very humble or too humble in one's feelings or actions."

17

AFFLICT

Afflict! Afflict! Afflict feels like being pricked. A thorn in the side! A prick! A thorn in the side feels like being afflicted. Both afflict and prick according to the dictionary means, "to cause pain or suffering, trouble, sting."

18

SOWING AND REAPING

One laments, "I'm so tired of trying to do things my way. Let go and let God! Have it your way, Lord; have it your way!" Malachi 3:8-10 complements this idea. It states that some harvest sown and reaped by laborers belongs to the Creator ~ God ~ Elohim: "Will a man rob God? Yet ye have robbed me. But ye say, wherein have we robbed thee? In tithes and offerings. Ye are cursed with a curse: for ye have robbed me, even this whole nation. Bring me all the tithes into the storehouse, and prove me now herewith, said the Lord of hosts, if I will open up the windows of heaven, and pour you out a blessing, that there shall not be room enough to receive it."

Does part of one's earnings, brought about from one's sowing and reaping, belong to the Lamb for the purpose of feeding his children? Yes! All the earnings from our labor belong to the Lamb. Out of one hundred parts of our labor, he desires us to give to him ten of those parts. It is from these ten parts he expects us to feed others. Remember the conversation Jesus had with Simeon Peter in John 21. John 21:15-17 states:

> Jesus: Simeon Peter, son of Jonas, lovest thou me more than thee?
> Peter: Yea Lord; thou knowest that I love thee.
> Jesus: Feed my sheep. Simeon, lovest thou me?
> Peter: Yea, Lord; thou knowest that I love thee.
> Jesus: Feed my sheep. Lovest thou me?

Peter: (Perplexed). Lord, thou knowest all things. Thou knowest that I love thee.
Jesus: Feed my sheep.

19

MUSTARD SEED FAITH

The size of faith can be compared to a mustard seed's size; and a mustard seed is very, very, very tiny. Remember when Peter offered Jesus a bid, a challenge? He wanted to know if it were really Jesus walking on the sea. He wanted to be challenged to walk on the water like Jesus. So Jesus told Peter, "Come." Matthew 14:25-31 tells the story.

> And in the fourth watch of the night, Jesus went unto them, walking on the sea. And when the disciples saw him walking on the sea, they were troubled, saying, it is a spirit; and they cried out for fear. But straightway, Jesus spoke into them, saying, Be of good cheer; it is I; be not afraid. And Peter answered him and said Lord, if it be thou, bid me come unto thee on the water. And he said, Come. And when Peter had come down out of the ship, he walked on the water, to go to Jesus. But when he saw the wind boisterous, he was afraid, and beginning to sink, he cried, saying, Lord save me. And immediately Jesus stretched forth, his hand, and caught him, and said unto him, O thou of little faith why did you doubt?

The significance of this story has to do with Peter's decrease in faith. It went from calling the thing, which be not a peaceful storm, as though it were a turbulent storm. When this happened, Peter stopped walking on the sea. When this happens to us, the loss of our mustard seed faith, we stop "walking on the sea." It takes unseen faith, not physical sight, to "walk on the sea."

What Peter should have confirmed, or confessed, was that peace and calm do exist in the midst of a storm, a circumstance, a situation. His thoughts about his circumstance, his storm, should have been held captive to the Master. Faith is evidence unseen, and the amount of faith it takes to believe in the unseen is minute—its size can be as little as a mustard seed. However, with use, faith's size increases, the same as a tiny mustard seed increases and produces a large plant.

20

TO BE OF GOOD COURAGE IS THE OPPOSITE OF FEAR

Fear is God's weapon to be used against Satan and is not Satan's weapon to be used against Elohim's children. Fear belongs to the one who is in-charge of a situation, and Elohim is in-charge of all situations and circumstances. It's been revealed that discouragement, or defeat, should not be allowed to come into one's heart. "One should hold thoughts of fear, of impatience, captive to me," says Jesus. Thus, one should only be fearful of Elohim and not of his enemy for whom fear was made. When one remains close to God and respects and keeps his Will, one will be judged, by Elohim, of being obedient. Malachi 1:6 tells who is to be feared: "A son honoureth his Father and a servant his mother: if then I be a father, where is my honour? And if I have a master, where is my fear? saith the Lord of hosts unto you."

Thus, one should fear the Lord and not one's circumstances. We should be of good courage always because good courage negates fear. The Spirit exhorts that one should be of good courage and be fearless. Joshua 1:19 states, "Have not I commanded thee? Be strong and be of good courage; be not afraid, neither be thou dismayed: for the Lord thy God is with the whithersoever thou goest."

21

GOD INHABITS PRAISE, OVERTLY AND INWARDLY

Perhaps the reason some people are timid about praising God overtly is that they don't want to be scorned by others. Yet some of these same people are unashamed to publicly exhibit their trust, their love, for their favorite sports team. God enjoys being lifted up by the people who trust, love Him, as sports heroes enjoy being lifted up by the fans who trust and love them. God's people are exhorted, advised, in Psalm 98:4-9 that all creatures should praise God by sometimes making a loud noise: "Make a joyful noise unto the Lord, all the earth: make a loud noise, and rejoice, and sing praise. Sing unto the Lord with the harp; with the harp, and the voice of the psalm. With trumpets and sound of cornet make a joyful noise before the Lord, the King. Let the sea roar, and the fullness thereof; the world, and they that dwell therein. Let the floods clap their hands: let the hills be joyful together Before the Lord: with righteousness shall he judge the world, and the people with equity."

Sometimes mediation is appropriate for praising God and may be opposite of making a loud noise to praise God. Joshua 1:8 states, "This book of the law shall not depart out of thy mouth; but thou shalt mediate therein day and night, that thou may observe to do according to all that is written therein: for then thou shalt make thy way prosperous, and then thou shalt have good success."

Surely, Elohim inhabits praise overtly and inwardly!

22

"WASN'T ADAM THE SON OF GOD TOO?"

This person who posed the question was not a proselyte nor a person who intended to change their faith from hers to Christianity. But this person was simply curious based upon the conversation she and I were having. The conversation was as follows:

Non-Christian: How can Adam be the first human to be created, be male, and not be thought to be God's son too?

Christian: Yes, Adam was the son of God too, but Adam was an extension of God. This is how all of humanity is related to Elohim—male, female, or eunuch—because we're all extensions of God, which means, we are all an image of God but not God himself. Thus, we creatures, male and female, and perhaps eunuch, are all extensions or creations of God, and Jesus, on the other hand, is not! Jesus is not an extension or creation of God because *Jesus is god!* This is the heart of Christianity: that God, firstly, is himself. Secondly, God is his Son who is named Jesus; and Jesus is the Christ, Christ meaning Savior of the world. Thirdly, and lastly, God is his Spirit given to humanity when he, in the form of his Son Jesus, rose from the dead and ascended into heaven to sit next to his Father as high priest. Jesus, as high priest, can be assessed by the righteous—can be cried to for forgiveness and for being saved from eternal damnation as a result of not repenting from continuing sin. Sorrow or repentance from sin is humanity's only access to Elohim. Good works alone do not save man from continuous isolation and departure from Elohim. Some have come to question if to believe that Jesus is the Son of God is a disconnect from repentance in terms of serving Elohim. Is one needed, and not the other, to follow Jesus? How likely is it that the rich man, who knew that Jesus was the Son of God, was unwilling to give up his riches to follow Jesus, at death, entered Heaven? Are they one, or are they two? To believe Jesus is the Son of God and to repent without compromise is necessary to be a follower of Jesus. Compromising that which is seen to be in agreement with the unseen is human but may be opposite of the Spirit.

23

SIN. TRANSGRESSION. BREAKING THE LAW.

There may not have been one man nor one woman at all. How humanity came to exist will always be questioned. Scientists believe in evolution while Christians believe in creation. There is an area of evolution or creation about which both agree, and this is that evil exists in the world. Never mind how it got here! If it got here through Adam or generations prior to Adam, the fact is that Christians do believe that evil ~ sin had to be conquered and was conquered through Jesus, through God himself ~ God's Divine Son. Christians believe that God had a plan for humanity's transgression ~ breaking the law ~ sin ~ disobedience. Salvation of humanity is achieved and conquered by one's belief in whom Jesus says he is, alongside resisting temptations which beset the flesh rather than lift the spirit.

24

FASTING. SACRIFICE.

Fasting itself is an offering ~ sacrifice to hear from God. The significance of an offering, a sacrifice, is to give up the physical for the spiritual. One dictionary defines "fasting" as the act of giving up one thing for the sake of another. This concept can be observed when the king of Nineveh decreed a fast among all the creatures of his population, humanity and beast, so that their cries and petitions would be heard. Jonah 3:4-9 states:

> And Jonah began to enter into the city a day's journey; and he cried, and said, Yet forty days, and Nineveh shall be overthrown. So the people of Nineveh believed God, and proclaimed a fast, and put on sackcloth, from the greatest of them even unto the least of them. For word came unto the king of Nineveh, and he arose from his throne, and he laid his robe from him, and covered him with sackcloth, and sat in ashes. And he caused it to be proclaimed and published through Nineveh by the decree of the king and his nobles, saying, Let neither man nor beast, herd nor flock, take anything: let them not feed, nor drink water. But let man and beast be covered with sackcloth, and cry mightily unto God: yea, let them turn everyone from his evil way; and from the violence that is in their hands. Who can tell if God will turn and repent, turn away from his fierce anger, that we perish not?

Sacrifice or offering has to do with giving up or planting seed to hear from God. In the Old Testament, animals were sacrificed for the purpose and expectation of one hearing from Elohim. In the New Testament age, seed, other than animals such as oxen or sheep, is to be planted. Sometimes, seed is called tithe. A tithe is ten parts out of one's harvest from one's labor. In order for a laborer to "obtain" a good harvest, the laborer must plant good seed. The good seed should be planted in fertile ground. Flawed or bad seed does not render a satisfactory or an abundant harvest; Elohim will judge the sower - laborer for sowing "bad" seed. Additionally, Elohim will not hold the sower - laborer responsible if the ground, in which the seed is planted, misuses the seed given. Misuse of God's seed may fail to bring about Elohim's will for his children. If the laborer thinks his/her good seed is being planted into or given to good ground, but it is not, this is not the business of the laborer. God will find grace or fault with the ground into which the laborer plants or gives his/her seed. The sower or giver simply plants or gives his/her seed and is not to judge how the "ground" uses it. How the ground uses it becomes Elohim's business and not the sower's or giver's business.

Sacrifice is what Elohim required of Cain and Abel. It is as to give up - to offer physical food to hear from God. Elohim liked Abel's offering better than Cain's offering because it represented the first part of the whole harvest. Genesis 4:4 calls this offering - this tithe a firstling. Genesis 4:4 states, "And Abel, he also brought of the firstlings of his flock and of the fat thereof. And the Lord had respect unto Abel and to his offering." Because it represented the first, it had no sin. Jesus is as a firstling, uncontaminated by sin. He is the firstling, a good seed, a perfect seed. He offered himself to God as a firstling, a perfect first. He was able to blot out the sins of humanity from the "eyes" of his Father Elohim. Consequently, humanity no longer needs an earthly priest to plead its cases before God, in terms of confessing their sins and asking forgiveness; but can go directly to God to plead cases, with Jesus as humanity's high priest/lawyer, because Jesus has already represented humanity when he resolved humanity's sins on the Cross.

It appears, sometimes, that the Old Testament talks less about love than the New Testament. Seemingly, the Old Testament talks mostly about the law or puts greater emphasis on the law. In the New Testament, Jesus's blood covers sin while in the Old Testament, the law covered sin. Additionally, because of Jesus's blood, the old law was shed for a new law, or the Ten Commandments was replaced by the New Commandment—love Elohim first, and love one's neighbor as one loves self. Hence, it is written that Jesus came not to destroy the law but to fulfill the law. He fulfilled it by covering it with his blood and giving us the new covenant when he gave up/sacrificed his earthly body and replaced it with a glorified body.

What does God want from me when I fast? God seems to say, "I don't want your money! I don't need your material possessions! Everything you own is mine anyway! The only thing which is not mine is your will. You must understand; I made you with a free will. My preference, or will, is that you choose me over sin/evil. But if your will is to do evil, or you choose evil over me, my will is to let you do what you choose to do. Doing your will instead of my will does bring about a departure from me. This departure does result in the need to repeat seeking me and finding my will. Continuing to fall away from me, disobeying my will, does complicate life much more than it should be complicated. It can even result in my taking away my desires for you and letting you 'do your own thing,' or do your own will, without trying to draw you away from your disobedience or change your mind if you choose to continually be drawn toward evil. This departure from me is as a reprobate."

Jesus's will is for him to lead you, but he won't lead if one doesn't want to be led or if one wills not to be led. He wants everyone to turn away from evil and to follow him because he is a Shepherd and desires to feed his sheep. Jesus is love, and his way is love. Love transcends hate, fear, promiscuity, restriction, and every other negative emotion which can be brought about, possibly, either physically or spiritually. In addition to contemplating the above, consider the fact that nothing belongs to us, but all things belong to God. Micah 6:6-8 tells us this: "Where with shall I come before the Lord, and bow myself before the High God? Shall I come before Him with burnt offerings, with calves of a year old? Will the Lord be pleased with thousands of rams, or with thousands of rivers of oil? Shall I give my firstborn for my transgression, the fruit of my body for the sin of my soul?"

So if God doesn't want from me any material possessions in order for him to hear me, because all of creation he owns, what is it God wants from me? One thing he wants is my confidence, and confidence translates to faith, trust, expectation, belief, hope. About confidence, 1 John 5:14-15 states, "And this is the confidence that we have in him, that if we ask anything according to his will, he hearth us: and if we know that he hear us, whatsoever we ask, we know that we have the petitions that we desired of him."

How am I to know God's righteousness? The Old Testament states that after having confidence, God requires the following, according to Micah 6:8. This verse states, "He hath showed thee, O man what is good; and what doth the Lord require of thee, but to do justly, and to love mercy, and to walk humbly with thy God?" To walk humbly with the Lord, in order to hear from God, has as its one element, repentance. The word "repentance," to many people, embodies a meaning which is cumbersome. However, it can be easy. To put it simply, repentance is to express sorrow. To say, "I'm sorry," with the intent of not repeating that action that's caused sorrow, expressing sorrow to Elohim, oneself, and/or to others. If one backslides or repeats the sin, it does not make one unloved by God, and it should not be unloved by others. God's love is not conditional. However, to continue to act on sin alongside continually lacking expression of sorrow, and without change, is disobedience. God, like our physical parents, does not like disobedience and does get angry and judge. Judgment can involve letting one do as one pleases with no conviction from God. Just letting a person or persons do as they please does result in a reprobate mind and make one likely to receive the second death.

God is not impatient with our actions. He waits for his children to change. He is patient. He perseveres and waits for sinners to turn toward him and away from transgression—wrong actions. Who defines transgression? Transgression is Bible-based if one has faith that Elohim hears. A lack of confidence that God hears, or that the validity of God's Word is not at all valid, could lead to disagreement, skepticism, discussion, or interpretation in order to prove that what God says is either the truth or untruth. Christians believe moral issues have been willed by Elohim and are not the business of politically correct courts to be decided, sometimes, by a higher court or a supreme court. Having said all of the above, fasting requires the knowledge that Elohim is patient and steadfast and does hear and answer confident prayers.

25

MONEY

Am I like a farmer in terms of money? The less seed I sow, the smaller the harvest? Sowing seed to a "beggar," someone who appears as impoverished who is begging for money on the street, always makes me feel a little uncomfortable because I question how the money will be spent. Sometimes, the money a beggar receives from me, I have debited from one of my two coffers, either my tithe or my offering. My questioning how the money I do give to persons in need was "laid to rest" by a drop of rain which relayed what is to be my response when I give or sow an offering, or a tithe, "It is God's business how the receiver uses the tithe or offering and not my business. He is the judge; I am not the judge."

26

FORGETTING, FORGIVING

God does not recall transgressions because of the shed blood of his Son Jesus. Prior to Jesus, transgression was remembered by him, and he required the sacrifice of animals—goats, sheep, oxen, etc.—to blot out transgression. When Jesus was sacrificed, because of his blood, his Father remembered sin no more. If God forgives debt—my debt—so should I forgive my debtors. How is it possible that I can forgive my enemy as Elohim gave and forgets sin? The way to forgive as Elohim forgave and does forgive sin is by requiring no "payback" and confessing Jesus to be the Son of Elohim and following Jesus. When Jesus came, he replaced evil for evil, which is as an eye for an eye and a tooth for a tooth, with love thy neighbor as you love yourself. Elohim's Word is not compromised when one loves the person, but not the person's action. Elohim is pleased when one acts obediently.

God wants people to know he hears. How does Elohim know people hear? His hearing is activated by the petitioner's confidence. Does the petitioner have the confidence, faith, belief, and hope that God will hear? What amount of confidence should be possessed by a petitioner in order for the petitioner to know God heard? How much time should pass between one's petition and Elohim's hearing? According to 1 John 5:14-15, if the petitioner has confidence, Elohim will hear: "And this is the confidence I have in him, that if I ask anything, according to his will, he heareth we. And I'd know he hears whatsoever I ask; I know that I have petitions that I desired of him."

Additionally, the petitioner must have patience. About patience, Isaiah 40:27-31 states:

> Why sayest thou, O Jacob, and speakest, O Israel, my way is hid from the Lord, and my judgment is passed over from God? Hast thou not known? Hast thou not heard, that the everlasting God, the Lord, the Creator of the ends of the earth, fainteth not, neither is weary? There is no searching of his understanding. He giveth power to the faint; and to them that have no might he increaseth strength. Even the youths shall faint and be weary, and the young men shall utterly fall. But they that wait upon the Lord shall renew their strength; they shall mount up with wings as eagles; they shall run and not be weary; and they shall walk, and not faint.

Jesus compared the size of faith to the size of a mustard seed. How significant is the size of faith when compared to the size of a mustard seed? Jesus told us that if one has faith as small as a mustard seed, that one should be able to move mountains. Matthew 17:20 makes this comparison: "And Jesus said unto them, because of your unbelief: for verily I say unto you, if you have faith as a mustard seed, ye shall say unto this mountain, Remove hence to yonder place; and it shall remove; and nothing shall be impossible to you. Howbeith this kind goeth not out but by prayer and fasting."

Certainly, hearing is activated by the petitioner's faith or confidence. One only petitions if one believes and has confidence that God will hear. One should always try to increase one's confidence. How is confidence increased? Through studying the Word, prayer, and fasting. Thus, fasting is important, alongside one's petitions or prayer, to hear from God.

Forgetting and forgiving! Forgiving and forgetting. They are both required of humanity by Elohim. How does forgetting and forgetting work? Forgiving is to stop feeling and acting angry over a situation or circumstance—a trial or tribulation. Is to be angry not being able to forget? Actually, anger is the antonym for forgiveness. So to not be angry, one must not be unforgiving. One must be forgiving to activate forgetting. One must love. Is forgetting love? God has forgotten because God is love. We too can forgive and forget like God because we've been made in the image of God.

27

PRAISE

Oh, how should I praise the Lord? I should say or speak good things about the Lord. I should speak positively of the Lord. For the words that are formed in my mouth and start in my heart, which I speak with my lips, should be praise. Literally, according to *Webster's Dictionary*, praise is defined to be, "to set a price on something or to figure out what a thing is worth. It comes from the Latin word for "praise." When we praise something, we are saying that we put a very high price on it. Additionally, to say good things about; to give a good opinion of."

Therefore, based upon what praise is, it is imperative that I should surely be aware that what should proceed from my mouth should be praises and blessings. Curses are unacceptable to God.

One's mouth is a mirror, in that it reflects the condition of one's heart—one's soul. David's heart must have been pure, evidenced by all the praises, credits, and honor given to Elohim in his Psalms. How should Elohim be praised? Elohim should be praised as he was praised by David in Psalm 33:

> Rejoice in the Lord, O ye righteous: for praise is comely for the upright. Praise the Lord with harp: sing unto him with the psaltery and an instrument of ten strings. Sing unto unto him a new song; play skillfully with a loud noise. For the word of the Lord is right; and all his works are done in truth. He loveth Righteousness

and judgment; the earth is full of the judgment of the Lord. By the word of the Lord were the heavens made; and all the host of them by the breath of his mouth. He gathereth the waters of the sea together as a heap: he layeth up the depth in storehouses. Let all the earth fear the Lord: let all the inhabitants of the world stand in awe of him. For he spoke and it was done: he commanded, and it stood fast. The Lord bringeth the counsel of the heathen to nought: he maketh the devices of the people of none effect.

28

SIN. THE OFFICE OF HIGH PRIEST. GOD'S PLAN TO SAVE HUMANITY.

Sin is personified in Adam. If Adam is a personification of sin, then righteousness is a personification of Jesus. Consequently, when I sin, I am sin; I become sin. Consequently, I must say I am sorry. To say one is sorry is the same as to repent. To repent or to say one is sorry is the same as to apologize.

Repetition of sin is evidence of the continual need to repent in one's effort to do better or become more right with God—more righteous! Evidently, to repent, to be sorry, or to apologize involves the spiritual heart in addition to the physical heart. If to repent moves one closer toward righteousness, then evidently repentance covers sin, replaces sin! When sin feels good to the flesh, when what is in the world feels better than what is in the spirit, it is harder to hear from God or the Spirit.

Before Adam sinned, there was no high priest because there was no sin among humanity. There'd been no departure from God because of man's disobedience; therefore, no high priest or lawyer was needed to plead one's case before the Father, Elohim, until after Adam's fall. With the advent of Jesus, brought by Adam' s disobedience to Elohim, humanity's transgression could now be forgiven. Jesus is a new seed, planted to replace the old seed, Adam. An appropriate petition follows:

God, as a result of your plan, a plan of redemption, I, like Jesus, although I am imperfect, desire to be a conduit. I'd like you to use the love which exists inside me to be a light to bring to others clarity and knowledge about your salvation. Let me remember to exhort others daily, as we are told to do by Paul in Hebrews 3:13. Lord, let me remember that love requires forgiveness and defeats evil. Hebrews 3:13 reminds me to take care that my spiritual heart remains believing and confident, so that I will desire not to turn away from Elohim. The Scripture reminds me to exhort everyone daily ·so that all others are uplifted and do not remain departed from Elohim by sin—continue in defeat. We all, through the defeat of the enemy by Jesus, became partners of Jesus; but, this is made possible by the confidence, trust, and faith we have in him to be the divine and only Son of Elohim and Elohim's present high priest.

Thank God, our sins are pardoned by a high priest, the Lamb who sits next to his Father Elohim, when we ask and when we repent!

29

FASTING AND WHY I SHOULD FAST WHEN I INTERCEDE FOR OTHERS

I can intercede better for others when I pray using these parts of prayer: thanksgiving, praise, and petition. These three parts, alongside fasting, are effective. They are effective because they bring a sacrifice to Elohim. Fasting can be compared to prayer because as prayer, it should give one a purer heart. God responds to a pure and sincere heart. A pure and sincere heart is as a sacrifice to God. We are and do become as a high priest, the purer the heart. We can come directly before God, through Jesus, with any petition since Jesus became high priest. We must come with a pure, sincere, and confident heart. No animal, other than self, need be presented as a sacrifice to God or act as a conduit for the ability to directly access the King. We no longer need an earthly priest to be able to access God because Jesus is presently the high priest, and through the name of Jesus, we are able to access God without a human, religious high priest, as had to be done in Old Testament time and prior to the Cross and resurrection of Jesus.

How is it that fasting is the same as bringing a sacrifice? Because through fasting, one's body becomes less defiled with impurities. Meaning, one's body become a clean vessel before the Lord. A high priest could not come before the Lord - intercede for - pray for the people without bringing a clean body, whether beast or human, like Jesus. This is a sacrifice! One's body, through fasting, becomes a cleaner, more fragrant body. Elohim is "yum-yum," and he wants "yum-yum" vessels. This was God's plan for the forgiveness of humanity's transgressions. God wants sweet-smelling, pure, clean, and holy bodies or vessels—bodies uncontaminated by sin, to be set before him, to adorn his sanctuary, church, and Kingdom. So the only body he could trust was his own. He knew that he was pure, clean. That there is no other way but his way that does testify to himself or the truth. He, and only he, is the truth. The truth does not compromise the Trinity. A miracle? Yes! A miracle because Elohim's Son's body became the perfect vessel with a 100 percent possibility of resisting temptations which leads to transgression or sin. Presenting his perfect body to his Father so that humanity's sins were forgiven, "paid for," and ransomed became the last animal sacrifice.

When Jesus's work was finished, he was assigned the role of high priest in heaven by Elohim. As high priest, he hears our intercessions and allows "fires," or trials and tribulation, which beset our lives from time to time, to be nonconsuming. He is the fire chief. The righteous are always delivered out of trouble even though they must experience trials and tribulations while living in fleshly vessels. The Word tells us repeatedly that nothing is impossible with God, and that Elohim oversees our trials and tribulations, and his will is done. Jesus sought his Father's will. Mark 14:36 states, "And he said, Abba, Father, all things are possible unto thee: take away this cup from me: nevertheless not what I will, but what thou will."

Like Jesus, King David also sought Elohim's will. Psalm 23:4 states, "Yea though I walk through the valley of the shadow of death, I will fear no evil: for thou art with me: thy rod and thy staff they comfort me."

Should the work of suffering, trials, and tribulations bring one closer to Elohim instead of driving one away from Elohim? Surely, Elohim remains with one through one's suffering and requires one's patience and perseverance as one waits upon the Lord.

Fasting brings about confidence. Confidence is as faith, hope in Elohim, which is increased by studying his Word. Where the Word is not studied there is less confidence, faith, hope, expectation, and trust. Faith is a work, an action. One can't have faith without doing the work; and doing the work is studying the Word. Consequently, faith without works ~ action is dead. The Word can be acted on by either of two ways, hearing or seeing. Seeing the Word involves reading. Expecting miracles to happen suddenly may cause one to be disappointed. Elohim is patient, long-suffering and persevering. Within his time, his will, and miracles will be done. Isaiah 40:31 tells us to wait upon the Lord: "But they that wait upon the Lord shall renew their strength; they shall mount up with wings as eagles; they shall run, and not be weary; and they shall walk and not faint."

We knew that to hear the Word, it can be best heard when one studies it, through listening to it, reading it, or digesting it. It can be digested through fasting for oneself and for others.

30

GIVING, SACRIFICE, FASTING, LOVE

Giving, sacrificing, and fasting can all be considered as synonyms. The sheep must feed the shepherd and the Shepherd, Elohim, must feed the sheep. The sheep should give gifts to the King ~ the Shepherd while the Shepherd gives gifts to the sheep. Consequently, the sheep and the Shepherd provide for each other.

Giving a gift or gift giving is a measurement. Sometimes, the greater appearing the gift seems to be, the greater can be the love. Consider the story of the widow and her mite which demonstrates a small gift or sacrifice but magnificent love. Therefore, is greater measured by sacrifice alongside abundance? God's gift to humanity came out of his sacrifice, his Son. It is unimaginable to not think that Elohim did not make a sacrifice because he did. Since the fall of Adam, God has used sacrifice as a way for humanity to draw closer to him. It is the way to be blessed by Elohim. In the Old Testament, pure blood from unblemished animals was sacrificed to God by high priests for humanity's sins, while in the New Testament, pure blood from God's Son, Jesus, was sacrificed to God; and Jesus consequently became the high priest. Animals in the Old Testament and Jesus in the New Testament were both seeds. Jesus interceded and does intercede as high priest of humanity.

God is not concerned about the amount or glitter of the gifts but the sincerity and righteousness of the giver's heart. The size of a gift may depend upon the size of the harvest. Additionally, what appears large to Elohim may seem small to humanity. Whereas, what appears small to God may seem large to humanity. God is concerned with the condition of the giver's heart, not the size of the gift. He desires humanity to have pure hearts, and he desires unblemished gifts to be cheerfully given. He has said, "Blessed are the pure in heart, for they shall see God." One's heart reflects one's unity with Elohim. Additionally, the first part from one's labor should be returned to God—one tenth since all things are his creations—his "stuff" to be planted and harvested. We should, alongside giving Elohim his portion, expect to care for our own needs, our family's needs, and the need of the "poor" with the rest.

For Solomon to have asked for wisdom and understanding reflected his unity with God and his willingness to be Elohim's good steward. The synonym for wisdom is to have a love for Elohim. The synonym for understanding is to walk close to Elohim and to never depart from him. Obviously, from the start of Solomon's labor, he'd approached Elohim with a pure heart and acted as a good steward of God's things by returning ten percent of those things he'd been given by Elohim through his physical labor to God.

31

LOVE OF MONEY IN RELATIONSHIP TO SACRIFICE

It doesn't seem like the love of money comes from having little money and wanting more, but its love may come from simply possessing it or having obtained it and one's desire to keep it from falling away. If you've only had little money or none at all, it has a short way to fall, and you just resume trying to "make a way," and you seemingly always persevere from lack. You depend on the ultimate Provider for help. Therefore, the lack of money may not be the love of money, but the love of money may be one is depending upon its ability to bring comfort: a desire to access those things—material possessions— which money can buy. One must beware not to put one's desire for things, for comfort, and for independence before one's primary support, which is Elohim. How does the love of money and greed relate to sacrifice? To "fast" means to give up, and "sacrifice" means loss or the act of giving up. Therefore, the desire to hoard or be greedy is contrary to giving up, sacrificing, or fasting. When one wants to hear from God, fasting may be chosen. Choosing to fast is good, but choosing to possess a contrite ~ right heart and to seek God first through fasting is best. To fast is to sacrifice. The blood from Jesus was the last blood God required to be sacrificed which would be needed to cover the sins of humanity. Yes, Jesus was the last Lamb! He was the last sacrificial lamb required for the sins of humanity!

Because he managed to achieve perfection, no other's blood will ever be needed to "hide" humanity's sins from Elohim.

To reiterate, the words "fast" and "sacrifice" are synonyms, or they have the same meaning. According to one's edition of *Webster's Dictionary*, the word "fast," as a verb, means to give up; and the word "sacrifice," as a verb, means the act of giving up. Jesus is our sacrificial lamb; at least he is for the ones who believe that he is who he says he is, the Son of God. Therefore, giving up something in exchange for something else helps promote a right relationship with Jesus, but it's not guaranteed. It is better to love others. Love is better. Micah 6:5-8 tells us that God requires a righteous heart, giving up something in exchange for something else or fasting ~ sacrifice. That those who desire righteousness must be just, loving, and kind. Consider this dialogue between Micah and God as inspired by Micah 6:5-8.

Micah: How shall I come before the Lord? Shall I bow? Shall I give in exchange for my transgressions, sins, and to stop your anger and appease you, calves a year old, thousands of rams, ten thousand rivers of oil, my first born?

God: I want none of these! What I want from you is righteousness. You don't have to give up ~ sacrifice ~ fast any material thing to hear from me, but righteousness comes from a righteous heart; and in order to get a righteous heart, you do these three things, none of which come from the physical ~ material. All of which come from the heart ~ the spiritual be just to others, love others, walk humbly before me, seek my will first. Put it before love of money, relationships, or anything else.

32

SACRIFICE AND FASTING

Through the death of Jesus, Jesus gave me something. What? He gave me freedom from the debt I owe to Elohim because of my transgression. He's like a bondsman, who pays a debt to the court, to the judge, and to the supreme authority, to keep the accused out of jail. Consequently, fasting itself is an offering ~ sacrifice ~ freedom. It is an offering ~ sacrifice based upon one's faith, expectation, confidence, love, hope, and trust to hear from Elohim and not primarily to benefit self. Hearing from Elohim should not be secondary to petitions to obtain things of the flesh. If Elohim is sought first, material provisions will abide. Therefore, I fast ~ offer ~ sacrifice myself to God not to pay a debt because his Son, Jesus, has already paid my debt to his Father; but I fast to recognize him as Elohim and acknowledge his mighty power.

To be mindful of the Creator's mighty power and omnipotence is to glorify Jesus as the New Testament law which embodies grace. Grace fulfills the Old Testament laws which embody "hard copy" rules and regulations. They are hard copy because the laws were written on stone instead of on the heart. Is it wrong to expect to receive from Elohim as a consequence of the act of fasting? No, it is not wrong, and 1 John 5:14-15 tells us it is not wrong to expect to receive from God petitions; but what is in error is to petition God for the things we want with lack of faith instead of with confidence. Confidence is as love and trust. First John 5:14-15 states, "And this is the confidence I have in him, that if I ask anything according to his will, he heareth me. And if I know he hears whatsoever I ask, I know that I have the petitions that I desired of him."

Basically, fasting should be an act to hear from God via a contrite heart. With a contrite heart, not only will self be lifted, but others will be lifted too.

33

FASTING ~ ATONEMENT AND DAILY SACRIFICE

When I fast, it is a sacrifice ~ an offering ~ an atonement; and according to a definition which is given in one dictionary of the Bible, "atonement" in a very simple term means, "to become one with God." Additionally, an edition of a *Webster's New World Dictionary* defines atonement as, "to make up for something done wrong." Through Jesus's death, evidence of both meanings of atonement can be seen. When Jesus was physically dead and was resurrected, he became one with his Father; and he made up for my wrongs done yesterday, today, and tomorrow. However, what must I do about my today's sins, or what must I do about the sins I do tomorrow? I must confess, even though Elohim has forgiven, does forgive, and will forgive, sin as a consequence of the Cross. The Cross makes daily repentance a way to save the soul, to renew one's soul. Consequently, salvation and renewal have been made possible with forgiveness and daily confession and repentance. What is the consequence of continual or habitual acts of sin or abomination? The consequence of sin is death resulting from continuing to act as a reprobate. One *Webster's Dictionary* defines the noun "reprobate" as a damned person or a very bad person.

Does reprobate infer that one is without a conscience based upon one's free will ~ choice? The *Dictionary of the Bible*, edited by James Hastings and revised by Frederick G. Grant and H. H. Rowley in 1963, talks about conscience stating, "The OT has no word for conscience; there, the sense of guilt and obligation is expressed in more general terms, e.g., 'David's heart smote him,' (1 Sam. 24:5, 2 and 1 Sam. 24:10) and 'My heart does not reproach me," (Job 27:6).

Regarding conscience and obedience to God the *Dictionary of the Bible* states, "For the NT, the sense of guilt and obligation which the common-sense language named conscience is a sign that each man is responsible to God."

The Bible warns that conscience is an index, or sign, of one being responsible to God for one's actions and still functions even in people who do not recognize its source. How is conscience, in terms of being reprobate, related to choice - free will? The Bible dictionary says that the sphere of conscience is choice in all its aspects, and that one's conscience may test one's loyalty to one's faith to the specific vocation to which one has been called by Christ. Consider Acts 23:1, 24:16, 1 Timothy 3:9, and 1 Corinthians 4:4. When Paul writes, "And Paul earnestly beholding the council said, Men and Women, I have lived in all good conscience before God until this day. And herein do I exercise myself, to have always a conscience void of offense toward God, and towards men. Holding the mystery of the faith in a pure conscience for I know nothing by myself, yet am I not hereby justified; but he that judgeth me is the Lord."

Does Paul's statement, "I am not aware of anything against myself," suggest a sphere of conscience? Is this his effort to help the population to whom he writes to discern right from wrong, good from evil, based upon one's conscience? The Bible dictionary says Paul confirms the sphere of conscience. The dictionary states, "Paul expects that God's judgment on each man—pagans included—will be confirmed inwardly by that man's conscience [when that man eats meat which has been sacrificed to idols (1 Corinthians 8:1-13)]." Was Paul's conscience activated when he discerned what he wrote in 1 Corinthians 8:1-13 about eating things? Some things being eaten had been sacrificed to idols, and this pricked Paul's conscience. Such consumption defiled these Corinthians. According to Webster's dictionary, defile means, "to make dirty or impure." The statement

Paul said, "I am not aware of anything against myself," does or could represent the verb related to the noun conscience. Is this his effort to help the Corinthians discern right from wrong based upon them knowing the difference between right and wrong via their conscience? The *Dictionary of the Bible* says, "Paul expects that God's judgment on each man—pagans included—will be confirmed inwardly by that conscience.

Romans 2:12-16 also confirms the sphere of conscience:

> For as many as have sinned without law shall also perish without law: and as many as have sinned in the law shall be judged by the law. For not the hearers of the law are just before God, but the doers of the law shall be justified. For when the Gentiles, which have not the law, do by nature the things retained in the law, these, having not the law, are a law unto themselves which show the work of the law written in their hearts, their conscience also bearing witness, and their thoughts the mean while accusing one another. In the day when God shall judge the secrets of men, by Jesus Christ according to the Gospel.

God desires proof that his product is ready to be used. Just as the world requires that all products must be tested before they go to market, God's children are tested before they're used. If you've never been tested, it's likely you won't be used regardless of your net worth. Consider Mark 10:17-23.

> The rich man asks Jesus how to live eternally: And when he had gone forth into the way, there came one running, and kneeled to him, and asked him, Good Master, what shall I do that I may inherit eternal life? And Jesus said, why callest thou me good? There is none good but one, that is God. Thou knowest the commandments, do not commit adultery, do not kill, do not steal, do not bear false witness, defraud not, honour thy father and thy

mother. And he answered and said unto him, Master, all these have I observed from my youth. Then Jesus beholding him loved him, and said unto him, one thing thou lackest: go thy way, sell whatsoever thou hast, and give to the poor, and thou shalt have treasure in heaven: and come, take up the cross, and follow me. And he was sad at that saying, and went away grieved: for he had great possessions. And Jesus looked round about, and saith unto his disciples, how hardly shall they that have riches enter into the Kingdom of God.

In order to inherit eternal life, one should have stood the test—overcome the test of trials and tribulations. Trials and tribulations, as strange as they may seem, do validate the purpose for life's existence and do provide strength for that existence as fire gives light—shine—brightness to unrefined gold. We are as gold! Elohim's creations do go through trials and tribulations, which do test one's ability in being able to achieve in life what God intended for one to achieve in life. Trusting in Elohim allows us to go through the fire, or fleshly temptations, without being consumed. One will eventually realize that sin may feel good to the flesh for a little while, but it will never satisfy without God's ~ Elohim's forgiveness. Elohim's will is for everyone's atonement or for all to become one with Elohim. Reprobate has to do with that which is false, or that which is opposite or unable to match or agree with Elohim's teachings or Word. Consider Jeremiah 6:27-30: "I have set thee for a tower and a fortress among my people, that thou mayest know and try their way. They are all grievous revolters, walking with slanders: they are brass and iron; they are all corrupters, the bellows are burned, the head is consumed in the fire; the founder melteth in vain: for the wicked are not plucked away. Reprobate silver shall men call them, because the Lord has rejected them."

The cross has made it possible to access Jesus prior to feeling the need to have to access a "middleman" or a minister, a pastor, a father, or a priest. The resurrection of Jesus, positioned ~ ordained Jesus as high priest, and it is to him we can, and should, go in order to bring our petitions before his Father Elohim and the Supreme Judge who sits in the highest court—heaven!

Jesus's act of dying on the cross can be compared to fasting. Why? When Jesus died, he gave up an earthly substance, his material body, for a heavenly substance, his spiritual body. He became one with God. Becoming one with God is an atonement, and he made up for humanity's wrongs. Jesus's atonement made it possible for humanity's sins to be forgiven by Elohim. Without the shedding of blood by Jesus, there could not have been an atonement. The shedding of blood signals imminent physical death because death is the loss of the body's lifeline or blood! Thus, in order for Jesus to act as an atonement for humanity, our lifeline had to be replaced with a new lifeline or Jesus's own. Jesus's atonement, or becoming one with Elohim, made it possible for man to experience a rebirth or be reborn by one receiving a blood transfusion from Jesus. One can receive this blood transfusion when one confesses Jesus to be the Messiah, the Christ, the Savior, the Lord, the Divine, and the Holy Son of Elohim. Fasting should allow one to connect with Jesus, to become one with Him. Physical food or blood is given up for spiritual food. Today, no blood need be sacrificed since Jesus's blood was given up. Him giving up his blood was, and is, the ultimate sacrifice. Becoming one with Jesus means one should petition God for anything, and he will hear. However, this petition should be done confidently and without begging, whining, or continuous repetition. Consider 1 John 5:14-15: "And this is the confidence I have in him, that if I ask anything according to his will, he heareth me. And if I know he hears whatever I ask, I know that I have the petitions that I desired of him."

Through fasts, one should expect yokes, or bonds, to be broken off oneself and others. Sometimes, fasts and petitions can resemble questions which do appear as debates with Elohim. God is made unhappy with such fasts because a prayer during a fast should not become a debate with God. Isaiah 58:14 states, "Behold, ye fast for strife and debate, and to smite with the fist of wickedness: ye shall not fast as ye do this day, to make your voice to be made on high."

Breaking the yokes, or bands, off self and others is a fast's purpose. When yokes are broken, it makes it easier for one to accept Jesus as the Miracle Worker, as the Son of God, as the High Priest, and as God himself. What yokes should a fast break off oneself and others? What yokes should be broken off in order to bring about freedom? Isaiah 58:6-7 answers this question: "Is not this the fast that I have chosen? To loose the bands of wickedness, to undo the heavy burdens, and to let the oppressed go free, and that ye break every yoke? Is it not to deal thy bread to the hungry, and that thou bring the poor that are cast out to thy house? When thou seest the naked, that thou cover him; and that thou hide not thyself from thine own flesh?"

What reward should one expect to receive as a consequence of fasting with confidence? Isaiah 58:9-12 answers this question:

> Then shalt thou call, and the Lord shall answer: thou shalt cry, and he shall say Here I am … and if thou draw out thy soul to the hungry, and satisfy the afflicted soul; then shall thy light rise in obscurity, and thy darkness be as the noon day: and the Lord shall guide thee continually, and satisfying thy soul in drought, and make fat thy bones: and thou shall be like a watered garden and like a spring of water, whose waters fail not. And they that shall be of thee shall build the old waste places: thou shalt rise up the foundations of many questions; and thou shalt be called, the repairer of the breach, the restorer of paths to dwell in.

34

REDEMPTION AND FASTING

The Book of Exodus, in which Moses is the main character, is about breaking. Breaking the yoke ~ redemption ~ being saved ~ rescued. Isaiah 58:6-8 tells us that fasting is to break yokes. It states:

> Is not this the fast that I have chosen? To loose the bands of wickedness, to undo the heavy burdens and to let the oppressed go free, and that ye break every yoke? Is it not to deal thy bread to the hungry and that thou bring the poor that are cast out to thy house? When thou seest the naked, that thou cover him; and that thou hide not thyself from thine own flesh. Then shall thy light break forth as the morning, and thine health shall spring forth speedily: and thy righteousness shall go before thee: the glory of the Lord shall be thy reward.

A drop of rain parallels Micah 6:7-8. It revealed that God desires one's heart and not one's material things. Humanity "suffers" from need and want, but God does not. When one gives one's heart to God, he'll bring about one's material needs and desires. Fasting is a way for one to give one's heart to Elohim or to seek him. Fasting is as a sacrifice when one gives up a thing to obtain things. The dictionary defines fasting as, "the act of giving up one thing for the sake of another." Therefore, one fasts for the purpose of hearing from Elohim. This is as a thing giving up a thing for the sake of another thing. The other thing is hearing from God. The thing given up is usually food, but the thing given up does not have to be physical, it can be spiritual. This latter thought paraphrases Micah 6:7-8. Micah 6:7-8 states, "Will the Lord be pleased with thousands of rams, or with ten thousands of rivers of oil? Shall I give my first born for my transgressions, the fruit of my body for the sin of my soul? He hath showed thee, O man, what is good; and what doth the Lord require of thee, but to do justly, and to love mercy, and to walk humbly with thy God?"

35

HOLDING BACK. FEAR. POSITIVE CONFESSION.

Holding back of any kind and for any reason is fear. Stepping out is faith. The evil one makes it seem as though the things Elohim gives don't exist without being tested with one's physical eyesight. However, God's invisibility does not negate his omnipotence or being. Science relies on things being seen. Since God is unseen, testing God lies outside of science. The enemy wants a confession that Elohim doesn't exist if he can't be physically seen or seen in the flesh.

To confess is to speak, to bring about something, a thing, as a result of using a specific language. A language is made with words. If words bring about a thing, how likely is it that one's confessions, one's words, do bring about the existence of things? The world was formed out of Elohim's confession ~ his word. His word, his confession, brought about the existence of all things in the universe. Elohim spoke, and all things were manifested. Similarly, as Elohim, when his children speak, things are manifested. Having confidence when praying to Elohim does bring about his hearing a prayer. Repetitive prayer may be evidence of a lack of confidence or fear of God not answering one's prayer. Fear is as unbelief and is a transgression when approaching Elohim in prayer. There must be no withdrawal from Elohim when one approaches Elohim. One's approach must be direct and without doubt. God rewards us for our lack of shame, doubt. He does hear us when we pray with confidence.

36

PROMISCUOUS

Opportunity has to do with chance. An opportunity, or chance, is to choose well or choose badly from a pool of choices or from a number of events, circumstances, or situations. To select without care from a number of choices or events, circumstances or situations is to select badly, or to take a risk. To select with care from a pool of choices, events, etc., means to not be promiscuous, to avoid a bad opportunity, or avoid a risk. To avoid promiscuity means to set oneself up for success—to have the opportunity to advance, to move forward. Promiscuity gives one the opportunity to experience a bad chance, to risk, or to fail. Consequently, friends should be chosen carefully. Being promiscuous means to not select carefully. Being promiscuous means to select friends and relationships without care. When Cornelius, according to Acts 10, was given an opportunity to select carefully and not be promiscuous, he chose carefully. He was obedient. Elohim used Cornelius's obedience to show that all people from every nation who call upon the name of Jesus shall be saved. Peter said to Cornelius in Acts 10:34 the following: "So Peter opened up his mouth and said: truly I understand that God shows no partiality. But in every nation anyone who fears him and does what is right is acceptable to him. As for the word that he sent to Israel, preaching good news of peace through Jesus Christ: (he is Lord of all)."

37

FIRSTLING

If you offer something other than the part of your "harvest," or your earnings, to the government, which the government expects to be paid, how pleased will Uncle Sam be with you? The government is never pleased when one does not give to it what it is owed out of one's harvest from one's labor. Like one's government being displeased when it is paid less than it is owed, so is Elohim. Elohim expects to be paid what is owed him out of the harvest from one's labor, or work. Elohim is never satisfied with second best. He doesn't honor a second, third, fourth, fifth, or sixth "best" offering. Offerings which appear "sick" as some sacrificial animals appeared in the Old Testament—sick goats, sheep, oxen—God does not honor. Giving such "sick" sacrifices to Elohim are disobedient acts. One's obedience to God generates him hearing and/or love acting on one's prayers or petitions. Regarding honoring Elohim Malachi 1:6-8 states:

> A son honoureth his father, and a servant his master: if then I be a father, where is mine honour? And if I be a master, where is my fear? saith the Lord of hosts unto you, O priests, that despise my name. And ye say, Wherein have we despised thy name? Ye offer polluted bread upon my altar; and ye say, Wherein have we polluted thee? In that ye say, The table of the Lord is contemptible. And if ye offer the blind for sacrifice, is it not evil? and if ye offer the lame and sick, is it not evil? offer it now unto

thy governor; will he be pleased with thee, or accept thy person? saith the Lord of hosts.

God requires a perfect sacrifice. Perfection pleases God. Additionally, obedience satisfies God. Whatever specifics he asks to be sacrificed should be acted upon.

38

OMNIPOTENCE. TIME.

You can't put God is a bottle. He doesn't exist between two points. He's not finite! He's infinite! However, if you want him, he can be found. Physically, God cannot be defined with the perspective artists use to define objects in their drawings and paintings because God cannot be defined with points. *There are no points with Elohim*!

39

LOVE

What is love? To understand the meaning of love, the following was revealed to me: God is not the verb, but the creator or noun or cause for the existence of all creations. Therefore, no verb or effect need follow God is, God is love. God and love are the same. Grammatically, "is" is a linking verb. It links God with the word love. Love can be an adjective or a noun which describes or names God. So "God is love" means a loving God or God is love. Therefore in actuality, love and God are synonymous.

Additionally, it was revealed that love is a measurement. A measurement of what? A measurement of how much one gives up. God gave up only his son—his life. The wealthy man, when told the way to find Jesus would be for him to give up his wealth, did not give up his material possessions, indicating what he loved most was his wealth and not Jesus. We should love Jesus first and things afterward.

40

A FORM OF WORSHIP

God hates sin. No imperfect person can stand before the Holy of Holies. So since we'll never be perfect, we'll always be as "filthy as rags." The only way we can enter the Holy of Holies is by belief in Elohim's Son since it was God's Son that took away our sins. It's Jesus who makes it possible for us to presently, and directly, enter the throne room—the courtroom of God—and stand before our judge, the Creator. Our belief in Jesus is what gives us this right. Jesus was made an additional authority at the time of his resurrection as a result of his perfection and sacrifice of his blood. We worship Jesus, the sacrificial Lamb. Repentance signals one's acceptance of Elohim's Word and of his Son Jesus being the real Christ, the Messiah.

41

FORMS OF WORSHIP:
TYPE OF WORSHIP

"You don't have to be beaten into submission for you to worship me," the prophecy revealed. This is a religious form, which some people prefer, and which others don't prefer. Ultimately, it's not the mode—manner of praise—of worship of the various denominations that causes a manifestation of Jesus in the lives of people; but it is the tenets of the Gospel, or Good News, of Jesus Christ. My acting upon the tenants causes my faith to increase, thus making it possible for me to be accepted into the kingdom of Jesus Christ. According to the Word, "Faith without works is dead."

An ultimate act should be the act of obedience in addition to realizing that God is a God of order. Consequently, as a result of my obedience and realizing that God is a God of order, I can hope and expect that things asked for, within the will of God, will be heard and manifested. God appreciates all forms of love given to him, quietly or with a loud noise. However, scripturally, loud shouts, loud cries, horns, and other musical instruments, dances, prophecy, and speaking in unknown tongues are all recognized as forms of praise and worship with a reminder that the greatest form of worship and praise is love. Love is the highest form of praise because all other forms do fade away. Love, too, is a gift. First Corinthians 14:1 says about this gift, "Pursue love, and earnestly desire the spiritual gifts, especially that you may prophesy."

42

FORMS OF WORSHIP: FAITH

Faith has to do with an understanding and knowing that God knows! He knows the unseen. He is the only fortune-teller on the sea and on the earth. He's seen and knows the past, alongside the present, and does know the future. He is omnipotent. He spoke creation into existence. His knowledge is superior to ours. Remember what he told Job and Job's friends when they tried to be judgmental or to propose hypothesis, theories, predictions about the reason why Job was experiencing this affliction, this trial and tribulation? God responded to this unbelief in Job 38:4. Elohim said: "Where wast thou when I laid the foundations of the earth? declare if thou hast understanding."

A drop of rain reminded me once, "Things are not always as they seem." Therefore, faith is the unseen and not the seen.

43

FORMS OF WORSHIP: THE SAVIOR

God's "thing" is about saving souls. God measures his wealth in righteous souls, contrary to the enemy whose wealth is measured in gold, silver, or other materials which, with the passing of time, are subject to rust and perishing. Whereas physical things impress the enemy, they do not impress the Savior, Jesus.

44

FORMS OF WORSHIP: THE CHURCH

God is. God is the church. The church is the existence of God. It should be an extension of God. The church is supposed to be evidence that God exists. It should bring about the proof that God exists. This was purposed by Jesus Christ when he brought about the existence of the church. Peter was, as are the righteous, an incarnate of the church. The church does not reflect nor have to reflect a building. It should reflect the condition or state of mind of an individual, of one's soul.

45

FORMS OF WORSHIP: WAIT ON GOD

The postponing of God's Word, in the form of an answer to my prayer, is not evidence that God's Word is not true, that there is no God, or that God doesn't exist. When I perceive hard circumstances, or situations, to be the result of unanswered prayer, then I set myself up for unbelief. Unbelief is sin, a transgression. The Old Testament provides evidence time and time again concerning Israel's anxiety and fear when God postponed an answer to their prayer. God had not answered their petition soon enough for them; therefore, they perceived this to be no answer. Consequently, they took matters into their own hands. This sin of unbelief caused them to have to be judged by God as being unrighteous.

The postponement of Elohim's Word should not make one fall away from Elohim or lack understanding about God's being, his character. Impatience reveals one's own character and not Elohim's. Elohim's identity is patience, perseverance. He has revealed this through the following prophecy, "Trials and tribulation develop perseverance, and perseverance must first finish its work (assignment) so that one can be made complete and whole, lacking nothing."

An additional prophecy revealed the same concept: "My daughter, my daughter, be encouraged, says the Lord. For you know it says in my Word. It says, consider it pure joy when you face trials of any kind because you know the testing of your faith develops perseverance, and perseverance must first finish its work so that you can be made complete and whole, lacking nothing."

If one has to give up things in order to worship the Lord, to seek the Lord in order to find him, then so be it. To wait upon the Lord, rather than pursuing things, may be a good act. Isaiah prophesied that they that wait upon the Lord shall increase their stamina, their faith. Isaiah 40:27-31 states, "But they that wait upon the Lord shall renew their strength; they shall mount up with wings as eagles; they shall run and not be weary; and they shall walk and not faint."

How will the Lord know how great one's faith is without having one persevere, or wait, on the answer? Maybe Elohim takes his time; he perseveres to test one's faith?

46

FORMS OF WORSHIP: RELATIONSHIP

Jesus should be central in one's worship, not denominational doctrine, which is a key concept in many forms of Christian worship. Without trying to interject the Gospel ~ the Good News with any other form of religious doctrine, the focal point of Christianity should be Jesus and the Holy Spirit. Establishing a personal relationship between oneself and Jesus is the single most significant requirement of being a Christian or Elohim's child. Water baptism is usually the first outward sign to testify of this new faith. It is a sign of repentance, and that one will try to walk in faith. Baptism by fire is a secondary form of baptism. It signals an empowerment that has been brought about by the Holy Spirit. It enables some individuals to worship Elohim by doing the following: utterance of wisdom, utterance of knowledge, dancing, healing, and miracles. Paul speaks of these gifts in 1 Corinthians 12:1-10:

> Now concerning spiritual gifts, brethren, I would not have you ignorant … Now there are diversities of gifts, but the same Spirit … For to one is given by the Spirit the word of wisdom; to another the word of knowledge by the same spirit; to another the Spirit of faith by the same Spirit; to another the gifts of healing by the same Spirit; to another the working of miracles; to another prophecy; to another the discerning of spirits; to another divers kinds of tongues; to another the interpretation of

tongues: But all these worketh that one and the selfsame Spirit, dividing to every man severally as he will.

But Paul, in 1 Corinthians 13:1-3, presupposes the following, "Though I speak with the tongues of men and angels, and have not charity (love), I am become as a sounding brass, or a tinkling cymbal."

Paul exhorts about speaking in tongues from 1 Corinthians 14:6-19. Basically, he infers that if a person speaks in tongues before a congregation, then it needs to be interpreted by that person himself or herself or by another person within the congregation, otherwise it is a useless noise. Speaking in tongues is meant to edify others as well as oneself. Paul states in 1 Corinthians 14:19, "Yet in the church I had rather speak five words with my understanding, that by my voice I might teach others also, than ten thousand words in an unknown tongue."

47

FORMS OF WORSHIP: DAILY SIN

To work out one's salvation daily was a phrase I heard as a child from various churchgoers as I sat in the church pew, listening to their testimonies. Then, I had no idea what it meant, neither did I give much thought to its meaning. Recently, however, I experienced a revelation which had to do with that old phrase, "Working out one's salvation daily." Salvation is a daily "work" because I'm always in judgment. Another way of saying, "I'm always in judgment," is to say, "I'm always walking in the wilderness because I'm always sinning." If my desire is to become more righteous daily, then I am being judged by God. So there will be no second judgment for the righteous because the righteous will already have been judged on earth daily, prior to their physical death, and will be judged righteous at the time of death. The righteous will proceed directly to heaven.

What kind of sin do I walk in daily? Basically, doing things to my neighbor that I shouldn't do or not doing things for my neighbor that I should be choosing to do. Consequently, my soul salvation must be worked out daily. It's a daily exercise. Exercising one's soul, or spirit body, daily includes or means confessing to God one's sin, then repenting or apologizing to God and apologizing to the person who was offended; and thirdly, trying to turn away from that transgression or to change one's behavior or actions. However, repetitive sin puts one in being a reprobate.

48

FORMS OF WORSHIP: SUFFERING

When this drop of rain was revealed, it told, "Suffering brings about a purging of every bit of sin we never even knew we had." Based upon this drop of rain, one might hypothesize that this is why many people experience suffering even to the point of death. Is it? Even coming into the flesh requires the mother's extreme suffering which brings about a very traumatic experience for the baby. Is this why Jesus had to suffer at the end of his life on earth, to bring about purging of humanity's transgression or to be the bearer of humanity's sins?

49

FORMS OF WORSHIP: THE WILDERNESS EXPERIENCE JUDGMENT

I'm always in judgment, walking in the wilderness, because I'm always sinning and not perfect or righteous as was Jesus Christ. I am not a holy person as was Jesus, but a sinner needing to work out my soul's salvation daily. Judgment is brought about as a result of my failure to keep Jesus's Gospel, "Love thy neighbor as thyself." Keeping this commandment will encourage one to treat one's neighbor, or other people, the way one wants to be treated. Walking through the wilderness because of one's sin mimics the Hebrew people's walk through the wilderness as a result of their transgression. Wilderness experiences, because of acts of sin, should be transforming and change one's behavior. God is merciful and desires confession and being sorry for one's sin.

Jesus is a warrior and with his priestly sword, he destroyed, does destroy, and will destroy evil. His word is truth. Regardless of one's sins, and regardless of one's trials and tribulations, there is assurance that repentance allows one to be inside Jesus and Jesus to be inside of one. This is the soul or the spirit person. The soul or the spirit form is separate from the physical form.

50

MANTLE AND REDEMPTION

Jesus's physical appearance, while he resided on earth, can be theorized. The reality seems to be that Jesus's origin began in the African/Edenic part of the world. The term African/Edenic is a term which has been used to describe the area of the world in which Jesus was born. The term is used by the Reverend Cain Hope Felder, PhD and editor of the *Original African Heritage Edition of the King James Version of the Bible*. If there is confusion about Jesus's physical appearance, it is traceable. Rev. Felder states in his editorial the following:

> What is the Bible? The most published book in the world is a historical record of the relationship between a particular people and "a particular God"; and how the specialness of that relationship has affected the entire world. The origin of this people has been shrouded in the mysteries of the various versions and translations of the Bible [especially the King James Version] for many years. This was due, in part, to the misinterpretations of those who recorded the original translations from Hebrew and Greek into Latin, English, and other Languages. However, a large part of the confusion stems from the deliberate Eurocentric attempts to conceal what today would be called the racial and/or ethnic identity of the people of the Bible.

The search is continued by Rev. Felder to find Jesus's true identity. He states, "Today, popular Christianity too easily assumes that modern ideas about race are traceable to the Bible or that there is not a significant black presence in the Bible ... Centuries of European scholarship along with a "save the heathen Blacks" missionary approach to Africans have created this impression."

It was Jesus to whom Elohim gave the mantle, making the redemption of humanity possible. This truth is more significant than the significance of his physical appearance while he was on earth.

51

JESUS IS THE HIGH PRIEST, REDEMPTION AND RECOMPENSE

This drop of rain has to do with redemption. The book of Exodus is a book about redemption, saving God's chosen people, the Israelites. Shem was one of Noah's three sons, and Shem's family came out of the Hebrew people who were the original inhabitants of the Garden of Eden or Africa/Eden as the Reverend Cain Hope Felder, PhD states. Rev. Felder is the general editor of the *Original African Heritage Edition of the King James Version of the Bible*: "Africa is actually of Latin origin and was imposed on that great continent by European explorers .... Because the term Africa and African are in common usage, we will employ them in conjunction with the terms Eden and Edenic. Many primeval groups migrated out of Africa, east of Eden." In fact, African/Eden was the source from which all peoples followed.

Abraham was Shem's grandson, and he was chosen from among other Hebrew people to leave his people and obey Elohim by moving to a different land. If Abraham and his people and his immediate family would obey, Elohim promised he would bless the family. The family would eventually evolve into a new nation. This new nation, subsequently, became Israel, whose inhabitants are sometimes identified as Jews. Abraham's son is Isaac, and Isaac's son is Jacob. Jacob was renamed Israel by Elohim, and out of his loins came the people of Israel, or the Jews, alongside the Hebrew prodigy Jesus the Redeemer and the world's High Priest. Jacob had twelve sons, one of whom was named Judah. It is from the tribe of Judah that the Redeemer came.

Before ten of the twelve tribes were "lost," ten tribes resided in Northern Canaan- Palestine; but the tribes of Judah and Benjamin remained in the Southern part of CanaanPalestine, or the Israelite kingdom in Jerusalem which held Solomon's temple alongside the tribe of high priests. Today, both Israel and Judah are being redeemed, alongside the redemption of non-Israelites or Gentiles. The current Jewish redemption was foretold in Jeremiah 30:3-4 and is referred to as Jacob's trouble: "For, lo, the days come, saith the Lord, that I will bring again the captivity of my people Israel and Judah, saith the Lord: and I will cause them to return to the land that I gave to their fathers, and they shall possess it. And these are the words That the Lord spoke, concerning Israel and concerning Judah."

Joel 3:6-7 also talks about Israel's redemption in the last days. It states, "The children also of Judah and the children of Jerusalem have ye sold into the Grecians, That ye might remove them far from your border. Behold I will raise them out of the place whither you have sold them, and will return your recompense upon your own head."

Israel's redemption is currently transcontinental. Lost tribes are being redeemed from more than one continent. Jonathan Bevins, the director of Jewish Voice Ministries, ministers to lost tribes. Regarding an Israel tribe living on the continent of Africa, called the Lemba of Zimbabwe, their claim to be descendants of the high priestly lineage of Aaron has been proven. *Jewish Voice Today*, the ministry's magazine states, "It's exciting for me to get this letter out to you immediately following our remarkable medical clinic outreach to what may turn out to be one of the largest "Lost Tribes" in Zimbabwe .... The claims of the Lemba had long been considered to be the stuff of legend— fascinating, but dismissed. Then, recent DNA testing revealed that an unusually high percentage tested matched the DNA signature of those known descendants of the high priestly lineage of Aaron, Moses' brother! Now the Rabbis and Israel are watching."

Regarding lost tribes being gathered from the continent of Africa, the Jewish Voice Ministry extends an invitation to join them when they go to Gondar Ethiopia to minister to Ethiopian Jewry. The ministry states, "Minister in the epicenter of Ethiopian Jewry-Gondar, Ethiopia. This city is where the Jewish community of this nation actually originated. Through a recent landmark change in Israeli Policy, Aliyah has opened to this impoverished Jewish remnant, and thousands are scheduled to return to Israel."

The European trade appears to have been an agent which surely distinguished the identity of the African/Edenic people among the Israeli population. If it did, what it seems to have done, it can be assumed that many Americans of African/Edenic descent have a Jewish or Israeli identity. Those Americans who appear as "African-American" or "black" could surely, and most likely, do come from various lost tribe of Israel, as the result of the European Transatlantic Slave Trade into South and North America and their respective islands. For years, the idea that black people, especially those living on the African continent, might be descendants of Israel had been disregarded and believed to be fantasy rather than the truth. Today, what had been regarded as fantasy is now proven to be truth. DNA testing has proven recently that one African/Edenic tribe, not in Northern African/Eden but in Southern African/Eden, is Israeli. The Lemba Tribe, living in Zimbabwe, Africa, has been proven to be descendants of the priestly tribe of Aaron as a consequence of DNA testing. Before this DNA testing, there existed no empirical evidence which proved the claim of the Lemba tribe to be Israeli, only speculation. Concerning this topic, Rev. Felder editorializes. This editorial appears as his footnote which parallels Joel 3:37. Rev. Felder states:

> This scripture concerns the African? Edenic Hebrew people into captivity. Historically, it is known that a majority of African/Edenic peoples who live in the Americas descended from ancient African/Edenic Hebrews who migrated after 70 A.D. across Africa/Eden over a thousand-year period ending up on the west coast of Africa. Many modern tribe of West Africa have

been documented to practice Hebrew Israelite customs, thus verifying their presence. The great European Slave trade that brought many African/Edenic peoples to the Americas had its beginning and concentration in West Africa. There are an untold number of black African Hebrews scattered throughout the United States. During the chattel slavery period in the new World African/ Edenic people were brought and sold without regard to personal needs. According to the definition if chattel slavery one is "totally" in the possession of another person and is used for private ends. There is neither control over one's destiny, nor control over the fate of the children. One is sold without regard to feelings, and may be ill-treated, sometimes even killed with impurity.

According to Jonathan Bernis, a lost tribe of Israel has been found living in remote Asia, in Manipur, India. He has written in his letter titled, "From the Desk of Jonathan Bernis," the following statement: "In just a few days, our largest team ever for outreach to Manipur, India, will leave with a clear mission that can't be delayed .... The state of Israel has announced that they will be bringing 1,000 members of the BneiMesnashe to Israel in the near future."

Additionally, Jonathan Bernis says that there is a large population of Jews living in Mexico who need to be reached so that they can hear about Jesus the High Priest and their redeemer. A *Jewish Voice Today*, published in March/April 2012, invites people to go to Mexico to minister to Mexico's Jewish population. The invitation states, "Mexico City is home to one of the largest Jewish communities in Latin America, numbering more than 75,000 Jewish People .... Come and minister to those who do not yet know their Messiah has come .... Be a part of history as God inspires these Jewish hearts through a celebration of Jewish history and heritage and challenges souls through the heart-changing Gospel of Yeshua."

The following are six individual statements which appeared in a children's magazine. They refer to Jews living in places outside

Europe. The statements provide evidence that Israel has always been known to exist in Africa/Edenic (which includes the Middle East) and Asia, Americas, and in Europe. The first of the six statement relates the following:

From ancient times until 1934, Iran was known as Persia. Every year at Purim, we remind ourselves how the Jewish people in Persia were saved by one of the Bible's favorite heroines—Queen Esther. While Jews have lived in Iran for centuries, many moved to Israel when the state was established in 1948. At the time of the revolution in Iran in 1979, some moved to Israel and the United States, while other chose Canada and Western Europe. There are thirty thousand Jews in Iran. Most live in Teheran and Shiraz.

The second statement states:

Cochin, in Southern India, is one of the world's oldest Jewish communities. No one knows exactly when the Jews arrived here. Some say it was during the time of King Solomon. Others think they arrived at the nearby part of Cranganore after the destruction of the Second Temple. What we do know is that, the first Cochin synagogue was built in 1344. In 1948, most of the twenty five hundred Jews in Cochin immigrated to Israel, leaving behind a Jewish community of fewer than one hundred. Cochin's magnificent Parades: synagogue, built in the 16th Century, is still in use.

The third statement states:

The history of the Jews of Ethiopia remains a mystery. What is certain is that they have lived in this African country for thousands of years, residing in mountain villages near rivers and streams. While most were farmers, a few were craftsmen working as tinsmiths and tailors. The Torah, which European Jews call "Orit," served as the center of their lives, and they kept many of its traditions. From November 1984 until January 1985, eight thousand Ethiopian Jews were brought to Israel in a secret mission called operation Moses. Later in 1985, Operation Joshua brought eight thousand more. The largest rescue—Operation Solomon—occurred on May 24, 1991, bringing another 14,324 Ethiopian Jews to Israel.

The fourth statement states:

Jews have lived in Turkey—originally called Anatulia—ever since the 4th century B.C.E., where they had prosperous and active communities. Centuries later, when news of the Spanish expulsion reached the Ottoman Empire, its leader—Sultan Beyazit II—issued a decree welcoming the fleeing Jews to his shores. Ever since, the Ottoman Empire and the Turkish Republic have offered Jews a safe haven from persecution. Today, the majority of Turkey's Jews live in Istanbul. Most are Sephardim. There are also Communities in Izmir, Ankara, Bursa, and Adona.

The fifth statement states:

Gibraltar's Jewish Community is a blend of Jews who fled from Spain and Portugal to England and Morocco [in the 15th century] and finally settled in Gibraltar, a peninsula on Spain's Southern Coast. The first Jews came in the 14th century. One hundred years later, all traces of Jewish life disappeared with the Spanish Inquisition ... In 1704, Britain captured Gibraltor, and in 1729, it signed an agreement with the Sultan of Morocco, permitting

Jewish merchants to return to Gibraltor. Today, there are only six hundred Jews there, but all of its original synagogues are still being used.

The Spanish Inquisition was one Inquisition among two other inquisitions, the Roman Inquisition and the Portugal Inquisition, which caused the Jewish population to leave Spain in the fifteenth century. The Spanish Inquisition was formed in 1478 by Catholic Monarchs Ferdinand II of Aragon and Isabella I of Castille and was meant to weed out heretics from within the church.

The sixth statement concerns Moroccan Jews:

> Jews have lived in Morocco for more than two thousand years—ever since Nebuchadnezar destroyed Jerusalem. Moroccan Jewish traditions ... reflect the history of that country. Jews began leaving Morocco for Israel when the state was established in 1948. From 1955 to 1957, more than seventy thousand Moroccan Jews emigrated. In 1961, Moroccan King Hassan II, gave the Jews the right to leave. Many went to Israel. There are only five thousand Jews left in Morocco.

Regarding Morocco, it is significant that Islam was carried to Morocco and other parts of Africa, especially the North, by its Arab neighbors from Arabia who are the followers of the prophet Mohammed. Today, Islam is the largest religion in Morocco, with more than 99 percent of its population adhering to it. The vast majority of Moroccans are Sunni, belonging to the Maliki School, according to the information provided on one website, Wikipedia. Wikipedia explains, "Sharia based on Maliki is the predominant Sunni School in North Africa, West Africa and parts of Central Arabian Peninsula. The Maliki is one of four major schools of religious law within Sunni Islam."

Lastly, in exploring the subject of Jesus as the High Priest and redemption and recompense, these words of Jonathan Bernis of the Jewish Voice Ministry are significant:

> My desire is to evangelize all people. When I go to the Jew first, I supernaturally reach more Gentiles than if I go to the Gentiles first. One example is my evangelistic outreach in Kaifeng, China. I learned that Jewish silk traders had settled in Kaifeng centuries ago. Before leading an outreach, I went to Kaifeng to "spy out the land." I found the remnants of an ancient synagogue as well as a number of Jewish descendants. Isaiah had prophesied that one day Jews from China would return to Israel. Isaiah 49:12 NKJV, prophecies Israel's return to their Promised Land. "Surely these shall come from afar; Look! Those from the north and the west, and those from the land of Sinim [China]."

Surely, Jesus is the high priest of both Israel and Gentiles. Both Israel and Gentiles having begun on one tree and having had its branches spread out to populate the earth.

52

PSALMS TO ELOHIM

These Psalms were revealed to me after a third day of a fast.

Psalm 1

The lord will order my steps and my family's steps, if we are obedient and depend upon him.

Psalm 2

The Lord will make us into righteous people if we depend upon him.

Psalm 3

The Lord will make us, me and my family, to have strong faith and belief if we just depend upon him.

Psalm 4

The Lord will help us, me and my family, find him if we just seek him.

Psalm 6

The Lord will give us our wants and desires when we ask, but when we ask, we must ask with no malice or hate in our hearts against ourselves or others.

Psalm 7

I thank you, Lord, that you have lifted the scales from my spiritually blinded eyes, and given us, I and my family, the ability to see physically.

Psalm 8

Let my family and I depend solely on you for comfort and not depend on the things or people of this world ~ things which belong to the enemy.

Psalm 9

Let me be loosed and freed by forgiveness, rather than being tied and bound or yoked by unforgiveness, hate, anger. Unforgiveness is anger and anger is hate.

Psalm 10

I thank God that I'm no longer blinded by what I cannot see. My sight depends on the God in me and not on the enemy outside of me.

Psalm 11

Let my family and I depend solely on you for comfort and not the things or people of this world. The things of the flesh will fail, but the things of the Spirit will live forever. Provide us labor so that we produce an abundant harvest for ourselves and others. Give us the patience and perseverance to stand throughout our labor. Give us the physical health, strength, and energy to stand. Be the rock which sustains us through hard circumstances ~ situations ~ trials and tribulations. Fill us with your joy and peace during "trying times."

Psalm 12

Lord, even if you choose or decide to take some or all of your, my, or my children's safety nets, lifelines, away at the request, urging of the enemy as he comes before you in your heavenly court, let us stand innocent based upon our repentance and sorrow for our sins. Let us live and be brought back to restoration. Restore our power, strength, prosperity, abundance, ability to forgive, faith, and love. Job lived and waited patiently on you to restore his health, money, shelter, family, and food. Because of his long-suffering, he received restoration. Lord, give me and my family the same perseverance during times of long-suffering, the patience to wait upon the Lord, because I understand that all things have been, are, and will be formed by Elohim. Lord, let us, me and my family, live to go inside the city as well as around the city. Take me into the throne room. Let me see and feel the manifestation of your power, your strength, and your glory. Let me tap your power, touch the hem of your garment as well as lapping your power ~ enfolding your power. Instead of being filled with scorn and contempt for me, you forgave me when I told you, "I'm sorry." My repentance brought about my repentance and yours. Let me be like Job, whom you told to not show scorn and contempt toward his friends because of their words, their accusations against him and you. Let my words, too, be merciful so that they bring about comfort and life. The Lord lets me decide who he is by his actions. How he acts, what he does, determines his personality. My faith in Elohim is based directly on his actions, as my faith in others is based upon their actions. Elohim is: the ordering of my steps, the Provider of my daily bread, the Giver of Life, my Savior from consuming fire, my Deliverer out of trials and tribulations, my Forgiver, the Repenter from wrath held against me, the Hearer of prayers petitioned with confidence, and the First Responder.

53

INTERCESSION AND MERCY

It is a sin against God to stop praying for others ~ interceding for others. Sure, Elohim is not pleased when I sin against him, but he won't forsake me because it pleases God to be my support to have created me; therefore, he forgives me. Since the Father is Alpha and Omega, "forgive" includes the past, present, and future. When others sin against one, it should not stop one for praying for one's enemy. Praying for one's enemy is the way to seek righteousness instead of committing evil ~ unrighteousness. Praying for one's enemy isn't an option; it's a command. To disobey Elohim's commands, without repentance, or seeking forgiveness, draws one further away from being lifted to heaven and nearer being descended to fire and brimstone. Samuel 12:22-23 expresses the above thoughts: "For the Lord will not forsake His people for his name's sake, because it has pleased the Lord to make you, His people. Moreover, as for me, far it be from me that I should sin against the Lord in ceasing to pray for you: but I will teach you the good and the right way."

Additionally, consider Ezekiel 3:16-21 when he is told by God to warn and intercede for the people:

> And it came to pass at the end of seven days, that the
> word of the LORD came unto me, saying. Son of Man,
> I have made thee a watchman: unto the house of Israel:
> therefore hear the word at my mouth, and give them
> warning from me. When I say unto thee, thou shalt

surely die; and thou givest him not warning, nor speakest to warn the wicked from his wicked way, to save his life; the same wicked man shall die in his iniquity but his blood will I require at thine hand. Yet if thou warn, the wicked, and he turn not from his wickedness, nor from his wicked way, he shall die in his iniquity; but thou host delivered thy soul. Again, when a righteous man doth turn from his righteousness, and commit iniquity, and I lay a stumbling block before him, he shall die: because thou hast not given him warning, he shall die in his sin, and his righteousness which he has done will not be remembered; but his blood will I require at thine hand. Nevertheless if thou warn the righteous man, that the righteous sin not, and he doth not sin, he shall surely live, because he is warned; also thou hast delivered thy soul.

The thing for which one prays may go unanswered when one most desires its manifestation. This does not negate the existence of the thing prayed to or Elohim! Elohim does hear prayers for ourselves and others, if one has confidence in him.

54

DON'T BE SO 'NOSEY'

If one asks Elohim to do a thing, than one should not concern oneself with how Elohim will do it, how he will act. If one petitions with confidence, then one can trust Elohim to act, and that one's request will be eventually manifested one way or another. Without one's confidence, love, and faith, Elohim does not hear; and one can expect one's prayer to go unanswered. Begging will not impress God, even when it is done out of faith, love, and confidence; and begging does not make him "hurry up"! Even if the answer, by Elohim to one's prayer, is not within our timeline or not when one expects, one should not be anxious for answers to prayer if prayers are done with faith, belief, hope, confidence, or expectation. Take one's nose out of Elohim's business, and afterward, like the lyrics of one song express, "Don't worry, be happy."

55

WISDOM, UNDERSTANDING. SPIRITUAL GIFTS.

Job 28:28 gives Elohim's definition for two words, wisdom and understanding. Are they discernment? Specifically, Job 28:28 states, "And unto man he said, Behold, the fear of the Lord, that is wisdom; and to defeat from evil is understanding."

Therefore, wisdom is fear of the Lord or the desire to love him while understanding is the desire not to depart from him. Together, they are as discernment. The scientific process answers many questions man has about the universe, but science can't answer them all. Science cannot explain the spiritual phenomena of wisdom nor understanding. This wisdom and understanding belong in the realm of spiritual gifts and cannot be obtained by any physical effort. They must be obtained through the spiritual because they are of the spirit. When one loves Elohim, it should bring about the desire—a longing to increase one's knowledge; a wisdom to seek, to study, and to know Elohim. Seeking him, studying him, does provide a surety about his presence, his being, his love. Love should translate into a desire to understand him, to develop a personal relationship with him by studying him—his Word.

Sometimes, it seems like what is given up in order to receive a "new" thing is not equal to the "old" thing which has been given up. However, this is not a question God should be asked. God is fair! He is the judge! He measures things out fairly. Remember, love is a measurement of the amount one gives up. God judges if what one has given up is equal to the amount received by one from God. Our responsibility is not to question the ways of God. He is fair. His scales accurately balance the weight it measures. God does not lie. God dislikes dishonest weights and scales. His justice is measured fairly—his love is measured fairly. Concerning understanding, a lack of understanding is a lack of knowledge about God, or a departure from the love of God. An unwillingness "creeps in" which make it more likely that one shall experience an increasing departure from God and making it less likely that one will experience a close relationship—a righteous relationship—with God.

An indwelling of love measured by how much is given up exists within each person. Gifts of understanding and love should be desired and requested by us of God. To not depart from God but to depart from transgression, sin, brings about wisdom and understanding. Where there is love, there is wisdom or fear of the Lord. Where there is understanding, there is a desire to not depart from him but to remain close to him by doing for others as we'd have others do for us. David illustrates this in his lyrics, Psalm 25: 12-14, "Who is the man who fears the Lord? Him shall he teach in the way He chooses. He himself shall dwell in prosperity. And his descendants shall inherit the earth. The secret of the Lord is with those who fear Him. And He shall show them His covenant."

56

EVIL ~ FALSE DOCTRINE. PEOPLE, THOUGHTS, AND CIRCUMSTANCES

Jude 1:8-10 basically is writing to the "church" about some people in the church being false prophets ~ promoting false doctrine. One is not to hold evil captive to the obedience of oneself or pay back others evil for evil. One is to hold evil thoughts, situations, and circumstances captive to Jesus. This relates to what Jude told the righteous to do when they were being mistreated and confronted by the enemy—the enemy being the unrighteous within their congregation. They were to hold their enemy captive, not to the obedience of themselves, but to the obedience of Jesus. He reminded them that even Michael the Archangel, when he was confronted by the enemy, held the enemy captive to Jesus and not to the obedience of himself. Jude 1:8-9 states, "Likewise also these filthy dreamers defile the flesh, despise dominion and speak evil of dignities. Yet Michael the Archangel, when contending with the devil he disputed about the body of Moses, does not bring against him a railing accusation, but said, the Lord rebuke thee."

Jude reminded the church not to try to repair or fix misguided members, which existed among them in their congregations, since God will administer justice. The desire to seek judgment is evil, not right. Love trumps "an eye for an eye and a tooth for a tooth."

57

THE LORD DESIRES TO HEAR FROM HIS CHILDREN. UNMERITED FAVOR.

It's Mother's Day, and as I try to wait patiently to hear from my grandson, I am reminded how patiently Elohim waits to hear from me and the rest of his children. Therefore, I should struggle to retain, to hold onto the gift of faith, regardless of the amount currently possessed. The petition has already been made by me for my grandson's welfare. I must be confident that Elohim's love is abiding. I must be aware that the petition for which I ask will be heard and will be manifested, received; but it will be manifested according to God's timeline and not mine. Consequently, I must act with patience, perseverance! I must believe in that which I cannot see physically, and that to not see physically is not evidence that it does not exist. Therefore, I should remain in good courage. I should be anxious for nothing. I am encouraged rather than discouraged by unseen situations or circumstances. I am reminded of what John states in 1 John 5:14-15: "And this is the confidence I have in him, that if I ask anything according to his will, he heareth me. And if I knew he hears whatsoever I ask, I know that I have the petition that I desired of him."

58

PRIDE

The following words and phrases all appear to have the same meaning.

1. pride
2. lifted up
3. proud
4. puffed up
5. lofty
6. exalt
7. holier than thou
8. know everything
9. authority
10. exceedingly great

These are all terms which should be assigned to Elohim, for only he should be lifted up ~ praised. He is the Creator. He is the Author, the Finisher, and the Judge. His creations, as am I, are only his messengers and not little gods, as some of his creations would like to imagine. Elohim is the Almighty One. He is wonderful. He deserves to be lifted up, praised, exalted, and titled the Holiest of Holy. The role of Elohim's creations is to be less prideful, less lofted up, or to not put self before Elohim.

I will lift up Jesus. I will be humble ~ consider myself a sinner and acknowledge my transgression or faults. Jesus is perfection. He is the First and the Last. He is the Holy One. Before him and others,

I will strive to be humble. I will be cognizant of the fact that to be humble does not negate my strength, my self-worth. It simply means to know one's own weaknesses and faults. To know one's own weaknesses and faults does not make one a thing to be scorned. Paul reminds us about reproaching what seems weak because what appears weak may be strong. Sometimes, the Spirit warns us that things are not always as they seem. Paul, in 1 Corinthians 12:6-10, states:

> For though I would desire to glory, I shall not be a fool; for I will say the truth: but now I forbear, lest any man should think of me above that he seeth me to be, or that he heareth of me. And lest I should be exalted above measure through the abundance of the revelations, there was given to me a thorn in the flesh, the messenger of Satan to buffet me, lest I should be exalted above measure. For this thing I besought the Lord thrice, that it might depart from me. And he said unto me, My grave is sufficient for thee: for my strength is made perfect in weakness. Most gladly therefore will I rather glory in my infirmities, that the power of Christ may rest upon me. Therefore I take pleasure in infirmities, in reproaches, in necessities, in persecutions, in distresses for Christ's sake: for when I am weak, then I am strong.

Hopefully, being humble will activate my love for others and activate me to treat my neighbor as I want my neighbor to treat me. Surely, I use Jesus as my support to give me the strength where I am weak, to feed his sheep.

There is a relationship between faith and humility. Faith is activated through prayer to the Creator, Elohim, in the name of Jesus. Through prayers, we ascertain a power greater than our own. Through prayer, selfishness can be exchanged for recognition of the welfare of others. We exchange our own will, pride for the will of another—the will of Elohim.

59

JUDGMENT

Habakkuk 1:2-8 states that the Lord prepares one nation against the other to administer judgment because of sin. One sin Israel had been using is found in Ezekiel 18:2: "What mean ye, that ye use this proverb concerning the land of Israel, saying, the fathers have eaten sour grapes, and the children's teeth are on edge?"

God corrects Israel by telling them that it is incorrect to hold the son responsible for the father's sin. Ezekiel 18:20 states, "The soul that sinneth, it shall die. The son shall not bear the iniquity of the father, neither shall the father bear the iniquity of the son: the righteousness of the righteous shall be upon him, and the wickedness of the wicked shall be upon him."

Is one generation responsible for the soul or sin of another? If so, some may want to know how one generation is responsible for the soul of another generation.

60

JOB'S DIALOGUE BETWEEN HIMSELF AND HIS FRIENDS

The cause for Job's adversity has been and will always be speculated. It wasn't up to Job's friends to accuse Job, to debate with Job about what sin he'd committed against Elohim, if any. After all, where had been Job's friends and Job when Elohim had created the universe? How is it that they knew more than God? They knew what God didn't know? Their questioning eventually seemed a debate and was a form of unbelief to God; and it grieved him. God confronted Job and his friends about their unbelief.

God made a way for Job and his friends to escape his judgment as a result of their unbelief. If Job would repent and ask forgiveness for himself, God would show mercy and spare his life.

If Job, too, would intercede for the unbelief of his friends, their lives would be spared. Therefore, this is what Job did. He asked forgiveness for his unbelief and the unbelief of his friends. God was merciful and alongside prolonging the life of Job and his friends, he returned Job's possessions, his things.

God has done the same for all of humanity. He gave mercy to the world through his Son Jesus. Jesus was the catalyst for God's forgiving humanity for its sin, thereby eliminating humanity from the certainty of spiritual death. When humanity turns from its transgression ~ repents, Elohim forgives—he repents.

Through the Cross, God has promised humanity's deliverance from hopelessness and despair. He has promised humanity a second chance. He has promised humanity mercy. In the story of Job, God shows Job how he must take hold of the promise if he wants to spare the lives of his friends alongside sparing his own life. Job's acts of forgiveness and intercession will bring about deliverance from pain and suffering for his friends alongside bringing about freedom from pain and suffering for himself.

61

I AM HEALED

Jesus, in his physical form, was unable to access every sick person on earth and heal them. But in his spiritual from, he can. Thank God! Through the Cross, Jesus "put off" the physical form for the spiritual form. Through the Cross, each of us, is able to experience physical healing through the name and spirit of Jesus Christ.

Should I believe God's Word about the enemy, that he came to steal, kill, confuse, and destroy and should not believe that God has healed through the Cross? Why can I believe God about the one unseen, the enemy, and I can't believe him about another unseen, himself alongside his Son and the Holy Spirit? How can I anticipate the appearance of the Antichrist and not anticipate the return of the Christ, Jesus?

62

JESUS IS PERFECT LOVE

Jesus is perfect love, and daily repentance ~ to say sorry is necessary, unless one has committed no sin within the last twenty-four hours. If no sin has been committed by one within the last twenty-four hours, then one can consider oneself to be perfect love like Jesus. However, no flesh is like Jesus's because all of God's creations fall short of being perfect love as a result of having sinned and/or them being disobedient against one's first parent ~ Elohim. Therefore, one must work out one's soul salvation ~ repent ~ apologize daily to Elohim, in the name of his Son Jesus.

Humanity should recognize itself as flesh and of needing to be "reborn" or delivered daily from evil to "good." Deliverance from transgression requires repentance. Jesus never sinned and never needed to repent. However, he repented from humanity's transgressions and not his own. Jesus never sinned and because of his perfection, He could redeem humanity from the second death. Elohim would not have accepted Jesus's blood as sacrifice for all humanity if it had not been perfect.

63

THE SIGNIFICANCE OF A STAFF

God is my staff. He sustains and supports me. This drop of rain parallels Ezekiel 29:6-7. Ezekiel is told by Elohim to tell Egypt's pharaoh that Egypt had been a staff of reed for Israel rather than a staff of support. Consequently, Egypt will be judged.

Is this the significance of Moses's staff? Did the staff represent Elohim's support? Physically, it may have seemed as a staff made of reeds; but spiritually, it was a staff made of far more superior materials than that of reed. The materials from which it was made supported Moses both physically and spiritually.

Monetary greed specially has an element of making one feel that money is like a staff and can be used for support or comfort. However, this thought is deceiving ~ false. Elohim is to be considered one's supports, not greed, nor other people. Seek God first for everlasting comfort, and he will bring about one's material needs and spiritual needs.

64

SEEKING COMFORT RATHER THAN BEING OBEDIENT TO GOD

God's answer to me and others about staying in Babylon and eventually receiving mercy was as the following. It had to do with not to seek comfort but to persevere through and in hard situations even if it feels very uncomfortable—to remain when it does not feel good to the flesh or good to the spirit. To remain in Babylon usually "pricks" both the flesh and spirit. Surely, it does not feel good to the flesh or to the spirit to patiently persevere in Babylon! It is, to say the least, very difficult to remain in Babylon without oftentimes feeling discouraged, anxious, or afraid. However, endurance does bring holiness. Patience ~ endurance represent obedience, and Elohim is activated by obedience. God's grace helps to accommodate one's patience.

The Lord tells the remnant of his people to stay in Babylon. But the remnant do not want to stay in Babylon with their captors. It is too hard! They want to go to Egypt, away from hardships and their captors. Escaper? Run away from their problems? Does escaping or running away from one's problems have a familiar sound? It's not easy to remain and stand stalwart in a hard place, an uncomfortable situation, or a hard circumstance. Like the remnant of Judah, most of humanity desires to go to a safe place—to be in comfortable spaces.

Jeremiah tells the remnant not to be afraid because Elohim's mercy will eventually be, but it will be according to God's will and not theirs. The remnant was expected to wait, to persevere, but they grew impatient. Jeremiah 42:16-17 relates this tale. It states, "If ye will abide in this land, then will I build you, and not pull you down, and I will plant you, and not pluck you up: for I repent me of the evil that I have done unto you."

The remnant desired their own will and not Elohim's will. They chose to leave Babylon, leave hardships rather than remain in it. They disregarded Elohim's repentance of the evil hardship they endured and his promise that he'd rebuild them if they'd be patient a while longer and persevere; to not persevere would mean they'd experience the consequence of being disobedient. Jeremiah 42:13-17 states Elohim's consequence:

> But if ye say, we will not dwell in this land, neither obey the voice of the Lord your God, Saying, No; but we will go into the land of Egypt, where we shall see no war, nor hear the sound of the trumpets, nor have hunger of bread, and there will we dwell. And now therefore hear the word of the Lord of hosts, the God of Israel; If ye wholly set your faces to enter Egypt, and go to sojourn there; then it shall come to pass, that the sword, which ye feared, shall overtake you there in the land of Egypt, and the famine, shall follow close after you there in Egypt, and there ye shall die.

Desiring a soft foundation and not a hard foundation as did Israel reminds me, somehow, of what a television minister said about discriminating between hard shell and soft shell creatures He said, "There is a Hebrew scripture which discriminates between mollusk-type creatures or creatures which are soft and without bone, a backbone; and creatures with a bone, a backbone. Unfortunately, the minister did not identify the scripture. Contemplating this statement, I realized that sometimes, hard things become soft, and soft things become hard; or that sometimes in life, the things which seem most difficult eventually become the things one and others most respect and treasure. This truth seems to affect both natural things and spiritual things. This was true about the remnant who left Babylon and went to Egypt. Their impatience negated their perseverance and obedience to Elohim and they left Babylon for Egypt. They sought a softer place. They eventually found that what they thought was soft, changed to hard. A situation they'd expected to be comfortable, without trials and tribulations, became difficult, not easy.

Is it possible or could it be that when circumstance rearranges one's comfort zone, one is better able to see one's purpose for life? Sometimes, just when it appears one has it easy, softer obstacles may come again and bring about one's awareness that what is needed to overcome trials and tribulations is patience and perseverance rather than a softer place or the need to escape or seek a different place.

65

GOD'S WORD IS TRUTH. SWEARING.

God has nothing higher than himself upon which to swear. Therefore, to use God's name as a word of reproach or profanity is unpleasing to Elohim and is not without consequences. Courts using witnesses to swear upon themselves and using God to be the helper is a backward tradition because man is not higher than Elohim; thus man, according to Elohim, can't swear upon himself. Only Elohim can swear upon himself or be sworn upon, but not man. Man is only the creation, not the creator. Isaiah 45:22-23 states, "Look upon me, and be ye saved, all the ends of the earth: for I am God, and there is none else. I have sworn by myself, the word has gone out of my mouth in righteousness, and shall not return. That unto me every knee shall bow, every tongue shall swear."

66

THE INHERITANCE. ITS SIGNIFICANCE.

When or if a father loves his children, he gives them an inheritance. This is what God ~ Elohim did because there is only one way to inherit the kingdom ~ the Father, and that is by the Father sending his Son. Hopefully, his Son is to be received by humanity. Hence, for believers or followers of Jesus, he is the way to receive the inheritance which Elohim promised to humanity as "payback" to him for humanity's transgressions against him. Transgression translates into disobedience. Man's first act of transgression was to desire Elohim's creations before desiring Elohim. Elohim is to be worshipped and not idols or things he created.

The enemy tempts humanity to seek self before seeking Elohim. Adam and Eve were tempted to seek self first, before seeking obedience to the will of God. One pays with death when one "buys" or engages in sin. That death does not pay for sin is what the enemy wants God's creations to be blind to. When Eve told the enemy, "We can eat the fruit, just not the fruit from a particular tree or the tree of life," the enemy did not deny that truth nor was his response deterred, he simply and matter-of-factly responded according to Genesis 3:34, "You won't die." The fact that their disobedience would not cause their fall or death was a lie. Hence, somebody's death would have to pay for my and your sin. If not an animal's death or sacrifice, a human sacrifice, or my personal death, then whose death? Whose death would pay for my sin? God ~ Elohim sent himself, through his Son Jesus to die. His death has paid for everyone's sin done yesterday, done today, and will be done tomorrow. Our responsibility for our sin is to confess it, bear forgiveness, or apologize. With our repentance, we can return before the presence of Elohim, and we will not have to experience the second death or spiritual death. Elohim's grace is not to be prevented. It is to march forward with truth and with our inheritance, Jesus. Preventative grace is Jesus, our inheritance.

67

HUMILITY VERSUS PRIDE

Humility is a term which suggests being humble or recognizing one's own weaknesses. To be humble is to be meek. To be meek indicates less self-pride to the extent that it does not negate the worth of others. Modesty is another term which suggests being humble. Arrogance, haughty, and puffed up are the terms which suggest pride, or holding a higher opinion of self than of others. God gives grace to the humble because he desires his children to recognize and care about others in addition to exercising boldness and good courage. He wants his children to exercise boldness and good courage and be anxious for nothing. Too many of God's children today are tempted to exercise pride over humility. When actually these two characteristics should work alongside each other ~ be in agreement. Too much of either discourages moving forward. Additionally, humility does not extract strength and should not be taken as a sign of weakness.

68

THE EVIL ONE

Since the enemy is Satan and he, the evil one, works through each of us to kill, steal, and destroy; this prayer is offered to God for one's defense and protection. Satan is the Hebrew word for enemy.

Prayer

Firstly, Lord, forgive me for unknowingly and knowingly "working" for Satan; and secondly, forgive others whom Satan has used to try to destroy my life. Lord, I pray for their salvation and righteousness. I pray that they find you as the right thing. You are the right word. I pray that we all seek you for a more righteous, holy heart. I affirm that the armor you told me to use for my defense against the enemy is the following, and I choose to wear it: confidence, right words or righteousness, perseverance, love, fear of you, obedience, and forgiveness.

Additionally, Lord, I desire to treat others the way I wish they'd treat me. Never mind payback! It is much easier for me to see someone else's faults or sin or "speck in their eye" than to see the speck in my own. Both the righteous and the unrighteous, Elohim gives a turn to receive judgment. The righteous receive the first judgment while the unrighteous receive the second judgment.

Let's take a look at Old Testament judgment, as it relates to payback. Exodus 21:23-24 states, "And if any mischief follow, then thou shall give life for life. Eye for eye, tooth for tooth, hand for hand, foot for foot."

Let's take a look at New Testament judgment, as it relates to payback. Jesus makes the following statement in Matthew 5:38-44: "Ye have heard that it hath been said, An eye for an eye, and a tooth for a tooth: But, I say unto you, that ye resist not evil: but whosoever shall smite thee on thy right cheek, turn to him the either, And if any man will sue thee at the law, and take away thy coat, let him have thy cloak also, And whatsoever shall compel thee to go a mile, go with him twain. Give to him that asketh thee, and from him that would borrow of thee turn not away."

Additionally, in Matthew 5:43-48, Jesus tells us we must love our enemy, the enemy is as workers of iniquity. Specifically, verses 43 and 44 state this command: "Ye have heard that it hath been said, thou shall love thy neighbour, and hate thine enemy. But I say unto you, Love your enemies, bless them that curse you, do good to them that hate you, and pray for them which despitefully use you, and persecute you."

69

WHY THERE HAS TO BE A TRINITY

Israel is God's inheritance to himself in addition to the remainder of humanity. He paid for humanity with his own blood. The blood to be obtained as a result of a bodily sacrifice needed to be pure and uncontaminated. Therefore, the blood could not come totally from the flesh. That part of the blood, which was flesh, came from the Virgin Mary. That part of the blood which was divine came from Elohim, Jesus's heavenly Father, the Alpha and Omega. When Jesus died, he left the Holy Spirit, which is the third part of Elohim or the Trinity. When Jesus is confessed to be the Divine Son of God by member of his humanity, that confession makes one become Elohim's inheritance. To become Elohim's inheritance makes one be saved. To be saved means one will not need to experience the second death or an everlasting departure from God.

70

MOONWALKING

Moonwalking may look cool, but it does nothing to move one forward. It just moves one backward. Backward to one's original starting point or further from the point one is trying to reach. One just returns to the point from which one's journey began.

71

PATIENCE

Most old people seem to be patient. Some may appear agitated, anxious; but mostly, they appear patient. Maybe they are patient because they have lots of time. They don't seem to feel rushed. God is patient. He is not rushed. Is this because he has lots and lots of time? Time is not an issue for God in terms of bringing about that which needs to be done, brought about, or created. Perhaps this is what the book of Job wants its reader to know. God gave Job lots of time before a cure was brought about which relieved him of his trial and tribulations, his spiritual and physical suffering. Though his tribulation, the time he spent during his hardship, he learned perseverance, patience. He had to continually remind himself, to convince himself, not to look at his dire circumstance; but to keep his mind on the Creator—to be patient! Eventually, the time he spent waiting on God, his patience, was rewarded. God obviously returned to Job, and Job received from God all which had been stolen—all that had been lost. Remember, time brings about patience, and time heals all things. What is the significance of patience, perseverance? Perseverance brings about holiness. It should draw one closer to God - bring about understanding. Understanding is as a proximity to Elohim.

72

THE REDEEMER OF ISRAEL

In whom should I believe? In whom should I put my trust? My trust, belief, faith, hope, and confidence should be put in the God of Abraham, Isaac, and Jacob. How should others know that the God of Abraham, Isaac, and Jacob is Lord? By receiving the Word that the Son of God, Jesus, was brought about by the biological fathers of the tribes of Israel or Abraham, Isaac, and Jacob. God created his chosen people, Israel, to be a witness of his existence. The destruction of his chosen people, through captivity, dispersion, or them being virtually annihilated, would make the God of Abraham, Isaac, and Jacob a deceiver. There would be no proof of the existence of the creator without his creations—his chosen people existing as proof of the creator's existence. As an example, historically, nations have tried to capture and destroy Jewish populations but have failed.

Even in the last days, before the return of our Lord, a remnant of people of Israel will be gathered worldwide, as a testimony to the existence of Elohim. Some Israelis from all the regions of the world will return to their original homeland, Israel. To pray and praise God acknowledges that Jesus is the Son of Elohim. All three, the Father and the Son and the Holy Spirit are as one. These three compose the Trinity.

As a redeemer, God, through Jesus, has repented and forgotten, and forgives our daily sins when we confess and ask God's forgiveness through his only beloved Divine Son Jesus Christ. Humanity's forgiveness has been brought about by Jesus's death and resurrection.

Humanity is given free will, free choice, to accept or choose Jesus to be the Divine Son of God and Savior from eternal death. To obtain this freedom however, it is man's or woman's responsibility to choose to repent or turn away from their sin and to ask Elohim's forgiveness. Repentance involves confession. Confessing one's sins brings about Elohim's forgiveness of the sin which the sinner has done to himself/herself or to others. This is to be unyoked, untied. Unyoking brings about freedom if the things to which one is yoked is problematic. Evil is problematic, and Elohim states in Jeremiah 42:10 the following: "If ye will still abide in this land, then I will build you and not pull you down, and I will plant you, and not pluck you up: for I repent me of the evil that I have done unto you.

We can prove the existence of the Redeemer and that he is truth by keeping his Word. The Holy Bible contains his Word!

73

NAMES ARE BLESSINGS

What's in a name? Names are blessings. Names can infer the blessing which has been bestowed upon one. Consider it a blessing to have a name which blesses because it could be highly possible that the name is and will be a mirror image of its owner. It is better to have been given a blessed name, than to not have been given a blessed name.

People should not be called "out of their names." Using names to call others something they aren't, God didn't intend others to be, could possibly open one to all kinds of destruction, devastation, or evil. Sometimes, the tempter just waits for the opportunity to lead one into temptation to call somebody out of his/her name, perhaps as a consequence of payback and in the form of anger for having suffered some loss. It's difficult to not submit to temptation in the natural.

Consider these names for God and their meanings (Hostings, James, *Dictionary of the Bible*, 1963):

El—originally it was not a deity's name, but a Hebrew word which references, perhaps, one who belonged to the tribe … once the tribe or migratory group was formed

El Shaddai—God almighty

El Roi—a God of seeing

Elohim—the ordinary Hebrew word for "God." It is found to be used as both a singular and plural form

Yahweh—means Lord. A personal, proper name used by the Jews as time advanced.

Adonais—later, Yahweh was replaced by the Jews for Adonais

God—the word "God" has not been found to be a product of the Jewish-Christian religion although it did exist in the Germanic family of languages in Pre-Christian times before some of the Hebrew people were called from among the general Hebrew population. The original sense of the word is doubtful but has to do "with what is evoked" or "what is sacrificed." Eventually, what is evoked or what is sacrificed was called "God" by the Jewish-Christian faith before the Hebrew-Christian traditions was established. As verified by the Bible, others called and continue to call what is evoked or sacrificed God, spelled with a big letter *G*, God. The general term is spelled with a small letter *g*, god. The religion one "uses," determines the difference.

74

THE TONGUE: THE POWER OF THE TONGUE

Let my tongue speak righteousness and justice and truth. Let my words bring joy rather than pain or sadness, success rather than reproach, and wellness rather than sickness. Let my words always add to one's character rather than subtract from it. Let my tongue praise God for being is. What is God? God is:

- just not unjust
- humor not sadness
- joy not depression
- love not hate
- courage not fear
- prosperity not lack
- a provider not a taker
- order not disorder
- unity not division
- freedom not yoked
- awareness not unawareness
- life not death
- a builder not a demolisher
- a communicator not a mute

- sighted not sightless
- a laborer not a slacker
- pure not impure
- a cornerstone not insignificant

75

GOD'S JUDGMENT IS FAIR

In God's eyes, we seem to be just the opposite of the way we see ourselves. We may see ourselves as poor and others rich. We may see ourselves as rich and others poor. According to God, if we want to be served, then we must become servants. If we want to be lifted up, then we must be scorned. If we want to be a big dog, we must learn or experience how to be a little dog. Regarding being the one being served, the big dog, and the one doing the serving, the little dog, Jeremiah 12:5 states, "If thou hast run with the footmen, and they have wearied thee, then how canst you contend with the horses? And if in the land of peace, wherein thou trustedst, they wearied thee, then how will thou do in the swelling of Jordan?

According to God, wealth seems to be equated with uplifting him and less equated with material wealth and possessions. This concept is seen in Matthew 9:11-13: "And when the Pharisees saw it, They said unto his disciples, Why eateth your Master, with publicans and sinners? But, when Jesus heard that, he said unto them, they that be whole need not a physician, but they are sick. But go ye and learn what that meaneth. I will have mercy, and not sacrifice: for I am not come to call the righteous, but sinners repent."

The above may help to answer the question about why some "good" people suffer and some "bad" people prosper. The answer might lie in the fact that God loves all his children. Might the condition of one's heart be more significant than the condition of one's wealth? One's material possessions cannot justify or judge the condition of the heart—one's righteousness.

Jeremiah 12:1-5 is a reminder of God's judgment. We should judge and love people because God loves. We should not let one's situation in life make a difference in how we treat others, judge others, and love others. Jeremiah 12:1-5 states, "Righteous are You, O lord, I plead with You. Yet let me talk to you about your judgments. Why does the way of the wicked prosper? Why are those happy who deal so treacherously? You have planted them, yes, they have taken root. They grow, yes, they bear fruit. You are near in their mouth but far from their reigns …. If you have run with the footmen, and they have wearied you then how can you contend with the horses?"

God loves all his children regardless of circumstance. He loves the footmen and the horses.

Additionally, the times in which we exist, whether they are hard or soft, should not be a condition for loving Elohim. Surely, it does not matter if one is in hard times or in good times; Elohim's love is not conditioned by trials and tribulations, by abundance or luck, nor by time. The Lord hears the prayers of righteous, and he gets tired of hearing. What then should be done? One minister, seen on television recently, asked this very question of Elohim and was told "Make a decision and I'll back it."

76

TITLES. SPIRITUAL GIFTS. CALLING.

Titles ~ spiritual gifts are not to be boasted about but should be used to bless others. One is what one is without it being boasted about. For example, one doesn't need to boast about the title of "bishop" because the fruit one produces will show that one is a bishop or show one's calling. Let God choose you, rather than the world.

77

HOW DO WE ENTER INTO THE LORD'S SANCTUARY?

How should one enter the sanctuary of the Lord? Thanksgiving and praise should be given in the presence of the Lord. Psalm 100:1-5 states: "Make a joyful shout to the Lord, all you lands! Serve the Lord with gladness; Come before His presence with singing. Know that the Lord, He is God. It is He who has made us, and not ourselves. We are His people and the sheep of His pasture. Enter in the gates with thanksgiving. And into His courts with praise. Be thankful to Him, and bless His name. For the Lord is good; His mercy is everlasting, And his truth endures to all generations."

78

LAND THE PROMISED NAMES

When Elohim sent Abraham out of his land, Ur, within the land of his birth, Mesopotamia, to a new land, it involved a name change for Abraham and later, a name change for his grandson Jacob. The name changes were necessary to reflect the men's character. Abram was renamed Abraham which means, the one chosen to produce Elohim's people or the one who crossed over from Mesopotamia to a new land ~ the Promised Land ~ Canaanland ~ Palestine ~ Phoenicia. Two generations later, Jacob, Isaac's son and Abraham's grandson, was renamed Israel. Jacob's twelve sons became known as the tribes of Israel. Out of the tribe of Judah, came Jesus. Sari, Abraham's wife, even had her name changed from Sari to Sarah by Elohim. I imagine this might have reflected her ability to have the child in her old age—the child who brought forth the tribes of Israel. The tribes of Judah eventually settled in southern Canaanland, which is Jerusalem, while the other tribes remained in northern Canaanland, or Palestine, alongside the tribes of Priests or Levi. North Canaanland was named Samaria and had a separate kingdom and king. After having experienced significant periods of dispersion because of political affairs, practicing Jewish populations are being identified to be living on every continent alongside those Jewish populations who were dispersed to Europe and live on the European continent. What is worthy of realizing is that a significant number of Africans, forcibly brought from Africa and enslaved in south, middle, and north America and their surrounding islands because of the

Transatlantic slave trade, can be included in the dispersion of Israel. Alongside Israel having been dispersed from the African/Edenic part of the world, to Europe and the Americas, Israel was dispersed into parts of Asia, China and India.

Sometimes, it is difficult to find the historical truth if names have been changed or borders have been changed. Changing names and borders makes it extremely difficult to find the identity of things. Things as specific persons, specific places, or things in general. Hiding things makes them hard to find. It's as playing the game hide and seek. But if we don't give up, we persevere, and we just keep digging, we might be able to win the game. Winning the game has been a significant purpose, apparently, for the editor Rev. Cain Hope Felder. He identifies the original identity of the names Jew and Negro in his editorial in the Original African Heritage edition of the King James Bible and has written the following: "In 1675 B.C. neither the name Jew or Negro existed. The term Negro was given to the Blacks as they left Africa for the slave ships (ca.1500A.D.). This is when the term "Negroland" was used. This is strictly a term coined by the Portuguese which means "black." It has nothing to do with a race of people. Using this term saved people from having to call slave, Cushite, Ethiopians or Abssynians, which they are sometimes called in the Bible."

Naming is significant for the identity of things. When names are changed, things become foreign. This concept that things lose their identity when things are misnamed can be seen in Rev. Felder's footnote. Because of dispersion, many Jews lost their identity. Rev. Felder stated, "The last great dispersion, in A.D. 135, was of the tribe of Judah, the largest tribe of Israel. Judah migrated across and through Africa for over a thousand years and most settled on the western coast of Africa. That area the Europeans named the "Slave Coast," or "Gold Coast" now comprises the independent nations of Ghana, Senega, Guinea, the Ivory Coast, Togo and Cameron."

Many of the customs of tribes of West Africa are similar to those of the ancient Hebrews of northeast Africa or the northeastern part of the African/Edenic region, renamed the Middle East. According

156

to Rev. Felder, the Ashanti of the Gold Coast forbade fighting on Saturday, the Hebrew Sabbath. They married inter-tribally only after performing cross-cousin marriages, and the Ashanti Hebrews wore a breastplate like the high priests of ancient Israel. Additionally, according to Rev. Felder, the Ashanti are an ethnically mixed people of West Africa, the ancestral home of most black Americans. Ashantis are closely related to the Fanti, Yoruba, Sudanee, and more distantly the Bantu. "The Ashanti tribes," states Rev. Felder, "Appear to have migrated from northern Africa, the "Middle East." Concerning this migration he writes:

> There seems to be a great mystery concerning the so-called "lost" tribes of Israel. The ten northern tribes of Israel, in 2 King 17, are said to have gone into captivity in 722 B.C., under the Edenic Assyrian King Schulmaneser, whose son was Sargon the Great. The tribes of Israel were placed in many cities in northeast Africa [parts of this African/Edenic region is now referred to as the Middle East]. One was Halah, a city of the Medes in Persia (modern Iran), where Israel intermingled with the cultures of the area and some Hebrews migrated to all parts of the Far East including India, Burma, and China taking many Hebraic customs with them.

What's in a name? The identity of people, places, and things. Unlocking the mystery of the origin of names provides great resolve to the "unknown." Currently, DNA seems to be a solution to solving this mystery.

79

WALKING BY WHAT IS NOT SEEN VERSUS THE VALIDITY OF FORTUNE-TELLERS

Everyone walks by sight unseen. Sight unseen means not knowing what will happen next, not being able to predict the future. Is this the reason some people seek fortune-tellers? They seek fortune-tellers because they desire to see the unknown; they desire to see what Elohim knows? Elohim discredits the use of fortune-tellers. Why? Elohim discredits fortune-tellers because only Elohim is Alpha and Omega, the Beginning and the End. God doesn't consult with any agent, other than himself, about the past, present, and future. Consequently, the "enemy" only knows the past. It's the past which the enemy does use or tries to use to convince us, to force us into believing that he/she knows the present and the future. Our present and future is only known by Elohim. The enemy has no part in one's future. Only Elohim knows the future! Therefore, one should never use one's past or one's present to predict one's future. Look upward! Praise Elohim that one's present or one's future is not necessarily linked with the past. Repetition of sin has been, is, and will be forgotten by Elohim when transgression is not repeated, and it is released from one through one's own sorrow or repentance. Through the sacrificial blood of Jesus, Elohim did make this possible.

80

GOD DOESN'T LIKE WHINING, SO BEG WITH CONFIDENCE— GOD IS LONG-SUFFERING

To say or beg in a whining way denotes the sentiment that one should please stop whining ~ complaining about one's troubles in a whining ~ complaining way. When we whine ~ beg God in a way other than with confidence hope, then we might be asking out of lack of hope and confidence rather than asking out of confidence. Expectation is brought about when confidence is exercised. When we petition Elohim with confidence, then we can expect our prayers to be heard. John 5:14-15 states, "And this is the confidence we have in him, that, if we ask anything, according to his will, he heareth us. Whatsoever we ask, we know that we have the petition we desired of him."

Consider the parable about the persistent woman. She can be likened to our consistently making a request to God, or repeating the request over and over again with persistence or begging. I believe her begging must have been out of a spirit of confidence, having faith in God, rather than a spirit of complaining, uncertainty, double-mindedness, "wishy-washy," or being lukewarm about God hearing her prayer, her request, because Elohim eventually did hear and manifested her petition. Lack of perseverance, impatience most likely, does bring about whining complaining ~ begging, signaling a lack of confidence, a lack of belief, or faith. Impatience is a childlike tool used mostly by children to get what one wants from their authority. These childish tools should be put away when one becomes an adult.

Elohim is patient, long-suffering. He perseveres, with humanity—patiently. It is with this patience, this perseverance, that he brings about his answer to his children's prayers; but his children's prayers must be confident. Recently, when I kept praying about the same situation over and over again, this response was given to me, "I get tired of hearing, so stand on the Word! This is your transgression, look not on the circumstance but me, the Word!" Not long after I was given this response, a similar response was given to a pastor I was listening to on television. The pastor wanted to know why his prayer had not been answered, and the response he got was, "I heard you the first time!" The pastor wanted to know what should be done and asked, "What should I do?" the answer came, "You decide and I'll back you."

The above two scenarios make us aware that God does not like whining and gets tired of us asking over and over again. If we ask confidently, with belief and with praise, then God does hear and always, "has our back"! Confidence is my giving without seeing that which I expect to see by my giving, my act.

81

REINCARNATION. BORN AGAIN.

The idea of reincarnation is synonymous with being born again. Born again can mean to be reincarnated. It may mean that I am in God, and God is in me. Not unlike the fact that the Father is in the Son, the Son is in the Father, and together the Third Person is created or the Holy Spirit. Jesus is an incarnate or an incarnation of his Father so is everyone who believes that Jesus is the Son of God.

Does the principle of reincarnation include the Word? Perhaps it's highly probable that its existence as a physical phenomenon can be debated because God is, and the Word is God!

82

SURETY

I'm so sure God, Jesus, and the Holy Spirit are one in me that I don't need to seek or find the Trinity in a church building. I can find Jesus in my heart. Jesus is in me, and I am in him. I should expect to find in a church building, however, an increasing personal relationship with Jesus Christ or a friendship with him. Unfortunately, currently, too many churches seem to be surety for establishing priorities other than to be surety for people's personal salvation or relationship with Elohim. Consider Judah! He was surety for his youngest brother Benjamin's life, as the church should be surety for one's life. Genesis 43:8-9 states, "And Judah said unto Israel his father, Send the lad with me, and we will arise and go; that we may live, and not die, both we, and thou, and our little ones, I will be surety for him; of my hand shalt thou require of him. If I bring him not unto thee, and set him before thee, then let me bear the blame forever."

83

THE WORD

It's probably better to let one's heart, the spirit, speak rather than letting one's mind, the flesh, speak. The most powerful things in the world are words. The Word was created with the Ultimate Word or Elohim. Genesis chapter one describes the world's things which were brought about by God's spoken Word. One should be careful to choose words to speak which bring life to uplift and not downgrade or bring their second death. The tone of words is important too. Words should remit kindness and gentleness, not hate. The word is like a two-edged sword. It can cut one and leave a lifetime scar. A cut can be bandaged, but it can still leave a scar. Some of the things which one can recall about deceased loved ones are the words of the deceased. Their words are left on tombstones, in books, in letters, in music, and on the mind and heart. Their words are as an inheritance.

Words can strengthen or weaken your relationship with Jesus. For example, when my deceased relatives come before me mentally, they come before me in terms of the word and the tone it carried when it was used during their time on earth. For example, one of my relatives always spoke, "God bless you," when something was done that she disliked. The tone of it always seemed to sound more like a curse instead of a blessing. One other relative spoke less accusingly. She spoke words of encouragement during easy and hard situations and circumstances. When I'd return home after having spent a long day job searching, she'd respond, "What did you suck, the lemon or the seed?" Unknowing which one I should have sucked, and am still ignorant until this day, I'd respond sheepishly, "I had a good day," or I'd say, "Things went well." Words seemingly, are helpful in a court of law or unhelpful. Words bind or unbind, yoke or set free, convict or loose

God is the Word. There was nothing that wasn't created, that wasn't created out of the Word of God. God is the Word! Words are our legacy to the world. Use them to uplift and bring hope, not punishment, despair, and discomfort. The word's tone should sound sweet, merciful, and joyful, knowing that our Lord is our Father; and all circumstances are under the obedience of Jesus Christ when we try to follow him or make choices which reflect his character, his personality. People don't deserve wrath, anger, because of another's desire to payback. Vengeance belongs to the Lord and is not personal. God has called humanity to serve and not to inflict judgment upon others with words. Psalm 33:9-11 indicates the significance and power of the Word. The Psalm states, "For he spake, and it was done; he commanded, and it stood fast. The Lord bringeth the counsel of the heathen to nought: he maketh the devices of the people of none effect. The counsel of the Lord standeth for ever, the thoughts of his heart to all generations."

Hence, the only thing left on which to stand in the world are our words! It is written in Psalm 34:13-14: "Keep thy tongue from evil, and thy lips from spreading guile. Depart from evil, and do good; seek peace, and pursue it."

84

BOREDOM. VANITY. SHYNESS.
A PURPOSEFUL LIFE.

Is continuous labor for the purpose of increase and consumption, like chasing the wind? Is to be bored like chasing the wind? There are two definitions for "bore" in a *Webster's Dictionary*. One definition is "digging holes." The second definition is "to make tired by being dull or uninteresting." Can digging a hole be compared to making one tired by being dull or uninteresting? One's life may feel spiritually tired as though it has been spent digging holes, or it has been made tired because of dull or uninteresting pursuits. One such event that may bring on "spiritual tiredness" is vanity. Is vanity a synonym for pride? One dictionary definition provides vanity as pride's synonym. If vanity, or to be vain, is a synonym for pride, then both are the same. Pride's definition, according to one dictionary, is, "an opinion of one's self that is too high; vanity.' Vanity, or being vain, can bring about the feeling that one's life has been worthless. Worthlessness is as having failed or not having experienced success, purpose, or value in life. Therefore, seemingly, the secret to having a purposeful life is not to be bored, which is to exchange vanity, high self-esteem, and pride with love and help for others.

Does extreme self-love, vanity, create a withdrawal from others, a shyness? Certainly, self-absorption leads to an inability to socialize with others. Surely, self-absorption, shyness, vanity, and pride makes one less appealing to others and may limit one's ability to experience physical, emotional and spiritual success and wellness to the degree one should possess and may desire. Is this what Solomon sensed when he said the following in Ecclesiastics 2:9-11: "So, I was great and increased more than all that were before me in Jerusalem: also my wisdom remained with me. And whatsoever, mine eyes desired I kept not from them. I withheld not my heart from my joy: for my heart rejoiced in all my labor and this was my portion of all my labor. Then I looked on all the works that my hands had wrought. And on the labor that I had labored to do; and, behold all was vanity and vexation of spirit, and there was no profit under the sun."

Alongside Eccleciastics 2:9-11, consider Jeremiah 2:5 which refers to vanity: "Thus saith the Lord, what iniquity have your fathers found in me, that they have gone from me; and have walked after vanity and are become vain?"

85

THRESHOLD

Threshold! The entrance into life! The extremely significant time in the period of growth and development! To enter life, after having been identified by the world as a child, as an adult! Consequently, children and childlike things need to be slowly removed from one's life to be replaced with more appropriate ideas, substances, and choices. At the threshold, the young man or young woman must learn how not to be promiscuous. This means they must learn to choose carefully. To select what one desires to possess with deliberate patience, perseverance, and care. Not being promiscuous will make it more likely that one will choose wisely.

86

BEWARE. RESPECTING GOD'S WORD.

If a synonym for beware is respect, than an antonym for beware is provoke. Respect versus provoke. Respect and provoke are opposite. In Exodus 23:20-22, Moses is told by God to beware of ~ to respect the angel instead of provoking or disrespecting the angel. Exodus 23:20-22 states, "Behold, I send an angel before thee, to keep them in the way, and to bring Thee into the place which I have prepared. Beware of him, and obey his voice, provoke him not; for he will not pardon your transgressions; for my name is in him. But, if thou shalt indeed obey his voice and do all what I speak; then I will be an enemy unto thine enemies, and an adversary unto thine adversaries."

In Ephesians 6:1-3, children are told to beware of or respect their parents by obeying them. It states, "Children, obey your parents in the Lord: for this is right. Honour they father and mother; which is the first commandment with promise; that it may be well with thee, and thou mayest live long on the earth."

Additionally, in Ephesians 6:4, fathers are told to be aware, to not provoke, or to arouse anger within their children—to not offend their children. It states the following, "And ye fathers, provoke [anger, offend] not your children to wrath [great anger]: bring them up in the nurture and admonishment of the Lord."

When I can respect Elohim's Word, or if I am aware of God's Word, than I am obedient to God or do not provoke Elohim, or do not provoke him to wrath, anger, or offense. Additionally, one must become aware or beware of the enemy who comes to steal one's joy alongside being aware of the presence of Elohim. Studying Elohim's word is what will make one beware and be aware of Elohim and his things.

87

HOW TO PRAY: THE THREE PARTS OF PRAYER AND THEIR ORDER

God should be praised because he is holy. He does right, and he is the only one who can administer punishment for our misdeeds. The fact that Elohim should be praised is the essence of Psalm 99. Psalm 99:1-5 sings, "The Lord reigneth; let the people tremble; he sitteth between the cherubims: let the earth be moved. The Lord is great in Zion; and he is high above all the people. Let them praise thy great and terrible name; for it is holy. The king's strength also loveth judgment; thou dost establish equity. Thou executest judgment and righteousness in Jacob. Exalt ye the Lord of our God, and worship at his footstool, for he is holy."

Having considered the essence of Psalm 9:91-5, I believe prayer can be expressed in three parts. These three expressed parts should be: sorrow or repentance, thanksgiving, and praise. The appearance of these three parts can be as follows:

1. Sorrow or repentance to express being sorry for one's transgression or sin. To know that forgiveness is available to one without having to die spiritually because of one's earthly sin. Some people choose not to believe this spiritual death. Jesus assumed this burden for humanity. His blood was given as a sacrifice for humanity's own impure blood. Consequently, one is able to confess one's sins, repent, and

feel sorry for doing them. The dictionary definition of the word "repent" appears in the *Merriam-Webster* dictionary. It means to feel sorry or to turn away from "new" sin and to resolve to reform one's life. In Psalm 38, David confesses and repents of his sin. David states that his iniquities have gone over his head, and that they are as a heavy burden and are too heavy for him. That his wounds will not heal properly because of his sin. In Psalm 38:17-18, he says, "I am ready to halt, and my sorrow is continually before me. For I will declare my iniquity; I will be sorry for them." Psalm 32 speaks of repentance or sorrow when it states, "Blessed is he whose transgression is forgiven, whose sin is covered."

2. Thankfulness. Be thankful as David is thankful in Psalm 16:5-6 for being part of God's inheritance and his favor.

3. Praise/Exhortation. Recognizing that it is God who saves one from one's enemies. David praises God in Psalm 18:3, "I will call upon the Lord, who is worthy to be praised: so I shall I be saved from mine enemies."

88

BETRAYAL

Betrayal means to fail to keep a promise, a secret, or an arrangement. Additionally, it implies being unfaithful, to forsake, to depart from, to give up, or abandon. In Matthew 27:46, Jesus asks Elohim, "Eli, Eli, lama sabachtani?" This phrase means, "My God, my God, why have you forsaken me?" This has been the question asked by a majority of humanity when trials and tribulations have been brought about by their own sin alongside not having been brought about by their own sins but by the sins of others. Regardless of what brings about trials and tribulations, they are as periods of moderate to intense suffering brought about by a known or unknown thing. A reprobate, or a very bad person, is considered to be a person who does not follow Jesus's way—a person who continues to practice actions which are displeasing to Elohim or a person who continues to become withdrawn from Elohim as a consequence of the acts he/she continues to practice which upset, anger, Elohim. Acts of betrayal or disobedience can be abominations if they are not stopped or changed and do lead to withdrawal from Elohim and death. Apparently, Eve believed the lie of the enemy; and instead of being obedient and faithful to Elohim, she ate the apple when the enemy told her she wouldn't die even though Elohim had told her she would die. Genesis 3:3-4 says, "God hath said, Ye shall not eat of it, neither shall ye touch it, lest ye die. And the serpent said unto the woman, Ye, shall not surely die."

Jesus made it possible for humanity to live when he purchased our sins from his Father God, Elohim, with his blood. Until that moment, humanity had been held hostage by our Father Elohim until he could be repaid fully for our sins. He had been paid with the blood of animals being sacrificed to him to repay him for sins; but when Jesus came and sacrificed his blood for our sins, his Father was fully paid for our sins—humanity's sins. Now regardless of what sins we commit daily, we are fully forgiven and have been since Jesus's death because his blood has been the payment for our sins. We don't have to die, but we can live and have eternal life when we go to God. However, we go to God though his Son, because his Son is the way, to daily ask to be forgiven for our wrong acts and the wrong acts of others. Sometimes, Elohim calls these wrong acts ~ abominations and sometimes, sin. Some of these wrong acts abominations sins are sexual (fornication, adultery, men lying with men, humanity lying with beasts, etc.). Others are not sexual: stealing, lying, slacking, and lust. However, the Gospel fulfils the Old Testament law, with Jesus's law, "Love thy neighbor as you love yourself." Regarding God's son Jesus being the way because he paid for our sins, Jesus now holds ~ owns our sins; thus, we must, when we petition Elohim, go through Jesus to get to the Father. Through Jesus, we ask to be forgiven by Elohim, and if we ask in confidence, Elohim will hear us. It is a fact that Elohim repented or changed his mind when he allowed Jesus to buy us back from Elohim with his blood. He's not only repentant in the New Testament but the Old Testament as well. Jeremiah 42:10 states, "If ye will still abide in this land, then will I build you, and not pull you down, and I will plant you, and not pluck you up: for I repent me of the evil that I have done unto you."

As Elohim's children, we are neither to betray or to expect payback from Elohim because of our betrayal when we tell him we're sorry for our abominations and do change our wrong actions or behavior. This is called forgiveness!

89

FORGIVENESS

If one desires to be a follower of Jesus, one should strive to be more righteous, holy. In order to become more righteous, sin must be wiped out continually. Nobody is exempt from sin. Either sinning oneself or being sinned against by another. Sin is covered by forgiveness. Jesus modeled forgiveness. He gave his blood to wipe out sin. Sin was covered by his blood. Consequently, Jesus's blood personifies forgiveness. To be forgiven is to have one's transgression covered. Transgression is covered when one repents. To repent is the same as feeling sorry. Confessing that some act which has been done by one is wrong, that it is a sin, it is a transgression, is repentance. Repentance cannot be brought about without the act of confessing. Confessing a wrong gives one the opportunity to repent, to become a righteous person; and not confessing or lack of confession and repentance can eventually heighten the possibility of a person becoming a reprobate. Forgiveness is a serving act. One who wants to be served by others needs to serve others. Forgiveness and serving are signs which point to the way. The way is Jesus, who is the High Priest and Messiah.

90

INVISIBILITY. OMNIPOTENCE. PERSPECTIVE.

The seen is always susceptible to being destroyed. The unseen cannot be destroyed. The Creator is the unseen. If he wasn't, how likely would it be that, like his Son, he'd have been crucified on the Roman cross? God, the Trinity, is an invisible entity; therefore, God is omnipotent. He is all things to all people; he is everywhere at the same time. His time is not our time, and he is timeless. Yet, his time, like the perspective in the landscape painting of a Renaissance artist, is not restricted. Perspective goes from one point to another point. However, like perspective, Jesus's invisibility brings about his ability to be at all points at the same time. He is omnipotent.

91

MONEY AND PERSEVERANCE

Things nor money to buy things don't glorify God. What glorifies Elohim is perseverance. What about when my money to purchase things is exhausted? Will I continue to glorify Elohim when my money becomes diminished or exhausted? Will I persevere? It is perseverance which establishes, builds, and brings about holiness, not money nor abundance or prosperity of things. One should be prosperous in perseverance! Ask Elohim to saturate you with perseverance which will sustain you during your times of trials and tribulations—through difficult time or through hard times.

92

SATAN'S BIGGEST LIE

A most effective lie of the evil one to cause humanity to fall away from Elohim, the Word, is to tell humanity that the Bible, Elohim's Word, is half-true or half-false. The following scenario illustrates the deceit of the enemy to make Elohim's Word seen untrue. A friend and I decided to do Bible study each morning via phone. The method chosen was to have one person read while the other person listened. After several sessions, two or three, I perceived that my partner was having difficulty following when I read from my Bible. The Bible from which I was reading was the King James Version. I asked her if she was reading, too, from that version. She responded, "What difference does it make? Man wrote the Bible anyway!" I was shaken but regained my composure and mentally affirmed, "Another attempt by the enemy to make Elohim a liar, a deceiver, false!"

93

IDOLATRY: ITS CONCRETE AND SUBTLER FORMS

There is a subtler form of idolatry than bowing down to wood and stone; and this subtler form of idolatry appears to include any act outside of Elohim's law or which by him has not been ordained. When 1 John 5:21 says, "Little children, keep yourselves from idols," about what idolatry is he speaking? John Hastings, the editor of *Dictionary of the Bible*, provides a clue in his dictionary that is a subtler form of idolatry. Hastings makes this statement: "Here the term covers all false doctrine and unworthy ideals which men may set before themselves, and by which their communion may be broken with Him."

Should all sin be classified as adulterous? Is any act which breaks any law of God idolatrous, false, or unrighteous? When the subtler form of the term idolatry is used, it appears that any act which breaks one apart from God is idolatry.

94

FAITH AND TRANSFIGURATION

The most effective followers of Jesus Christ study his Word! Reading the Word establishes and builds faith which is the foundation of his Word. Unless the followers of Christ study his Word, they'll be ineffective followers. Through the study of the Word, the evidence for faith is seen. Faith is unseen! It is to know and to have confidence that God keeps his Word. Without studying God's Word, it is impossible to learn that he keeps his Word. If I want to know that God keeps his word, I must study his Word.

To know that there is a Jesus Christ, and that he is the Son of God, has nothing to do with having had him exist physically on earth. It does have to do with the cross and having had him to be a sacrificial offering for humanity's sin. This is called transfiguration, or the replacement of sin ~ the old body for a new holy body; and transfiguration was brought about as a result of the Cross. Christ became a new creature. He was transfigured or changed. His sin body, as a consequence of Adam's sin, was replaced. It was replaced with a holy body, a glorified body, a transfigured body, a new creature. Thus, he became a new creature in God. No longer was part of him a creature outside of God—a creature outside of God's will. This departure has been brought about by the first man's and the first woman's disobedience which translated into transgression or sin.

As a result of his transfiguration, mankind was brought back to God. As creatures having been brought back inside God's will, humanity is now able to personally approach God without the aid or help of an earthly priest. God can be accessed via the High Priest, his Son Jesus Christ. Through the Cross, Jesus became the high priest and sits on the right side of Elohim to advocate for humanity. Therefore, direct rather than indirect access to Elohim is now possible through the name of Jesus. One can go directly to the throne of God with one's prayers, petitions, needs, desires, will, hopes, and expectations without intercession from an earthly advocate or priest. However, when one goes, it must be with confidence! Without confidence, it is highly likely that one's prayers may go unheard. Why? Because faith or confidence is the catalyst which causes God to hear and to support us when the petitioner acts on God's Word. Prayer, when it is not acted on through God's Word, cannot be acted on if one does not affirm the Word of God.

One should know there is Jesus, the Son of Elohim, not because one can or cannot see him with one's physical eyes, but because of one's confidence in his existence. If he exists, than one can be confident that he hears! Does Elohim's hearing depend upon one's degree of faith? Also, does faith come by hearing? Also, does faith die when it is not put to work or when one does no labor which brings about petitions being manifested?

95

FIXING A SPIRITUAL HEART ATTACK

If one has thoughts of sickness, acute or chronic, broken bones, or specific illnesses, one should put on hold those thoughts under the obedience of Jesus! Why? Because anytime one is praying for healing, one's own healing or another's healing, the enemy can put thoughts into our heads, but he cannot read one's hearts ~ thoughts. The heart is of the Spirit, and it is where faith and confidence are birthed. Faith can be made larger when one studies Elohim's Word. The enemy uses fear, the very weapon Elohim created to be used against his enemy and not for the enemy to use against Elohim or his creations. One should hold those thoughts which are contrary or disobedient to Jesus, to his obedience. This is as fixing a spiritual heart attack.

96

THE IDENTITY OF JESUS
THROUGH THE VIRGIN BIRTH

One can or should believe in the virgin birth and believe that Jesus is divine or that he is the Son of God. This is to be Christian or a follower of Jesus, but one cannot believe that Jesus is not the Son of God, as a result of the virgin birth, and still be a Christian or follower of Jesus. Consider John 1:18 and what it states about this concept: "No man hath seen God at any time; the only begotten Son, which is in the bosom of the Father, he hath declared him."

To be a Christian means many things to many people. Christianity is segmented or divided into many parts or elements. However, Christianity only has one way; and that way is Jesus. Consider what Jesus did in order to be identified as the way. He offered himself, his perfect body, for humanity's transgressions! He became the lamb to be offered to his Father as a payment for humanity's sins. Consequently, he became the high priest, making it possible for humanity to bypass earthly, fleshly priests, to come directly before the throne of Elohim to seek forgiveness. Without forgiveness, there would not have been nor is there any way for humanity to be saved or not to die. To be saved is to escape the second death into fire and brimstone. Revelation 20:14 says, "And death and hell were cast into the lake of fire. This is the second death."

97

GLORY: MY GLORY VERSUS GOD'S GLORY

Glory. Importance. To boast in the glory of self rather than to boast in the glory or importance of God or to not give Elohim credit for being important or to not praise him indicates pride or a prideful heart. Remember Isaiah 9:9-10. The prophecy states, "That say in pride and stoutness of heart, the bricks are fallen down, but we will build with hewn stones: The sycamores are cut down, but we will change them to cedars."

98

LORD, SHOW ME HOW TO LOVE MY ENEMIES

Lord, it is not my will but your will for me to love my enemies. My flesh, my humanness, brings about my stubbornness to freely not love my enemy. It is much easier to see the fault in my enemy's eye than in my own eye, such as selfishness, unbelief, hypocrisy, pride, undisciplined, ambivalent, etc. I know I must love my enemy or those unlike me or those I dislike because it is Elohim's will that unity exist among all his Creations. Therefore, I strive to do and act accordingly to Elohim's will and plan for my life. Never mind the flesh, I must rely on the word of Elohim which he has placed in my heart to do the right thing—to love my enemy. When I serve and not judge, I can best follow Jesus and Elohim's will for my life. When I serve and not judge, I will treat my enemies the way I will for my enemies to treat me. This is love!

99

RULES VERSUS CHOICE

One religious community, according to a television show, allows its children when they reach adulthood to leave the nest or the community to experience life outside of its confines. To do so provides them the opportunity to experience life without a set of rules being imposed on them by the religion practiced inside the community. To leave the community means they can make their own choices and not be yoked by the choices of their parents. It means nothing is forbidden, and there are no restraints. Nothing is off limits, and they can choose to desire anything according to their personal will.

With the birth of Jesus came choice—freedom. This is not to say that with the birth of Jesus, in the New Testament, that the law of the Old Testament became obsolete. This is to the contrary because the birth of Jesus fulfilled the law and did not do away with it or make it obsolete. Rules and laws are as signals. Just as traffic lights help cars and pedestrians navigate streets, rules help people to select to navigate right choices

100

"HOLD THOSE THOUGHTS CAPTIVE TO ME," SAYS THE LORD.

One should not try to do it oneself, solve ones problems alone; but one should solve problems, situations, circumstances as Michael the Archangel solved his situation. He chose to solve his problems with Elohim's help. Jude 1:19 states, "Yet, Michael the Archangel, when contending with the devil he disputed about the body of Moses, durst not bring against him a railing accusation, but said, The Lord rebuke thee, to act according to prophecy."

101

TIME, GOD'S OMNIPOTENCE, AND THEIR RELEVANCE TO GOD'S HEARING

Humanity is very aware of time especially when time requires having to be waited on. One usually wants to hear from God immediately. Sometimes, God is an immediate God; and sometimes, he may not be. However, God is never late, and he's always on time. Judging God or unrepentance of sin against God is not a smart move to make. Patience and perseverance are smart moves to make when waiting on God. Doing what one wants to do out of impatience or not being able to wait on God has consequences. Regardless of the consequences, they can move one away from God. Feeling faint while one waits on God is human. However, one should act with good courage and not be anxious or faint. God knows all about one's troubles, one's trials and tribulations; and he does answer. Just wait! He created time and one's desires should be left in his hands. God is time, he is omnipotent, and he hears when one believes or has confidence. He hears.

102

WHY WE PRAY IN AN UNKNOWN TONGUE

Praying in a human language is so inadequate because these prayers are for men to hear alongside God's hearing. Followers of Jesus should ask for the gift of speaking to Elohim in a language only known to Elohim. When this happens, this is called speaking in tongues. We need to be helped to speak in tongues. Jesus promised to humanity to send a helper when he physically left this earth, and he did send a helper. The helper he sent is called the Holy Spirit ~ the Holy Ghost ~ the Comforter. The Holy Spirit is the third part of Elohim's Trinity. Elohim's Trinity consists of himself, his Son Jesus, and his Holy Spirit.

The Holy Spirit helps believers speak directly to God in God's language. Speaking to God in God's language gives the petitioner an advantage. The enemy cannot decipher God's language or tongue. Speaking in tongues is as a hedge for God's children which protects them from the enemy. The speaker in tongues can more fully know Elohim's purpose for his/her life and even his/her destiny. Consider this message, which was sent in this drop of rain, concerning speaking in tongues. This drop of rain was not delivered to me but to someone else. It stated, "Satan cannot read our thoughts, he can only put thoughts into our mind which he wants us to act on so that they will cause damage or loosen our grip on the truth, the truth where our power and strength derive."

The following drop of rain was delivered to me concerning speaking in tongues, and it brought forth the following information:

> To confess is to speak, to bring about something, a thing, as a result of using a specific language. A language is made up of words. If words bring about a thing, how likely is it that our confessions, our words, do bring about things, events, whether they are good or bad? The world was formed because of Elohim's confession. His Word brought about the existence of all things in the universe. Words or language can be thought by the mind or spoken by the tongue. Words, create language. Words exist in the mind alongside existing in the tongue. What's in the mind or mouth is geminated in the heart.

103

CHEWING ON THE WORD: A SECONDARY DROP OF RAIN

THOUGHTS ON THE BOOK OF REVELATION

Write the vision, and make it plain upon tables, that he may
run that readeth it. For the vision is yet for an appointed
time, but at the end it shall speak; and not lie: though it tarry,
wait for it, because it will surely come, it will not tarry.
Habakkuk 2:2-3

MY JOURNEY

Consider Paul's "journey" in Galatians when he tells his purpose for writing the letter to the church in Galatia. His purpose has not been to exhort, to preach a gospel different from the one he preaches; but his purpose is for the gospel he preaches to be known that it has been received by him from God, and that it has not been taught to him by men. Galatians 1:10-12 states, "For do I now persuade men, or God? For if I yet pleased men, I should not be the servant of Christ. But, I certify you, brethren, that the gospel which was preached of me is not after, man. For I neither received it of man, neither was I taught it, but by the revelation of Jesus Christ."

Chewing on the Word (COW) seems for me to be a similar journey. My intent has been to not exhort but to deliver the Word of God with clarity and not that which is after man. However, it does not sequence all the events of Revelation, especially Revelation 20-21. Nor does it attempt to explain the meaning of symbols as is so often done during exhortations. If COW does anything, it should make you think! Changing its word will skew its contents; its whole thought!

COW'S PURPOSE

Chewing on the Word, or COW, brought about this secondary drop of rain to the original *Drops of Rain*. Cow is a thought about the book of Revelation. It does not change Elohim's Word, as it was given to John in Revelation. It appears to complement John's Book. It is as its title "Chewing on the Word" and is to be chewed on. Hopefully, COW will bring about a clarity about the Lamb's last days.

COW'S IDENTITY

"Chewing on the Word" was assigned an adjective to identify its assignment. This identification was assigned by a drop of rain which came: "This book is sacred." The definition of sacred, as defined by a *Merriam-Webster* dictionary alongside its synonyms, are these:

- devote exclusively to one's service or use
- worthy of veneration or reverence
- of or related to religion
- blessed
- divine
- hallowed
- holy
- sanctified

Its identification has not been changed, and its identification should not be given a new assignment.

AN EXPLANATION OF
THE DIVISIONS OF
THE BOOK OF REVELATION

The Holy Spirit in "Chewing on the Word: a Secondary Drop of Rain" seems to have divided the Revelation of his coming into four parts. A division of which I personally have never heard nor seen be done by scholars and/or exhorters who talk about, have explained, or do explain the Book of Revelation. After its fourth division, Jesus returns in Revelation 20 and the Tree of Life returns in Revelation 21. Nevertheless, the Holy Spirit explained Revelation to me in terms of the following sequence.

1. A Period of Tribulation. This is a period, a time, a season in which we are going, but maybe one in which we've existed or been in since the fall away of Adam and Eve from God; and one in which we will be coming out of, soon, according to the Word given to me. Tribulation has two parts, parts A and B:
    (A) The Tribulation Period: the Condition of Religion.
        Revelation 1:1-ca5:13
     B) The Tribulation Period: After the Condition of Religion.
        Revelation ca6:1-ca.8:1

2. A Period of Wrath ~ Anger.
    Revelation ca8:1-ca14:18

3. Period of Harvest.
   Revelation ca4:19-ca19:10.
4. Period of Judgment.
   Revelation ca 19:11-21,
   Revelation 20:1-15

A synopsis follows COW's four divisions with the anticipation and expectation that it does and will bring about clarity to this drop of rain titled Chewing on the Word or COW.

TABLE OF CONTENTS

Drop of Rain's Chewing on the Word

Division 1-A

The Tribulation Period:
the Condition of Religion

Revelation 1:1-ca5:13

1-A. The Tribulation Period: the Condition of Religion. Revelation 1:1-5:13

Rev. 1-3   Religious practices take preference over having a personal relationship with Elohim. Church ~ organized religion ~ doctrine ~ denominations ~ religious practices have agendas other than putting Elohim first.

Rev. 4   Elohim is worthy! He is worthy of worship and is to be worshipped. He is King and Creator of the heavens and the earth. He is Alpha and Omega. He has created, is creating, and will create all things. He is ultimate knowledge and, because he is ultimate knowledge, he is omnipotent. His omnipotence causes him to know and understand everything. He is not limited by space. He is space and is in every space, every place at the same time. Additionally, because Jesus the Lamb completed his assignment on earth ~ did his Father Elohim's will to save humanity from second death, he is Elohim; and Elohim is he. He is in Elohim, and Elohim is in him. The Holy Scriptures completes and complements the Trinity within the two. Because the Father, Son, and Holy Spirit compose the Trinity, they give the Lamb knowledge to the future and its mystery—the mystery of the Father, Elohim.

Revelation 5:1   A book written and on the back sealed with seven seals.

Revelation 5:7   The Lamb took the book out of the right hand of him that sat upon the throne. The Lamb, because he is successful in returning humanity to Elohim, is rewarded by being given the keys to the kingdom.

Thus, the Lamb, like his Father, now knows the future, knows the mystery. The little book with the seven seals represents the span of time on earth known as the tribulation. This period is also often referenced as Elohim's wrath. It is not the same as the period or season of wrath because it is still within the tribulation period. The tribulation period does not end until Division B, the Tribulation Period: After the Condition of Religion in Revelation 8:1-5:13, ends.

Elohim's Wrath ~ Anger, within this Division B: Tribulation Period or the Tribulation Period: After the Condition of Religion, in Revelation 8:1-5:13, is humanity's tribulation and has been brought about by the selfish desires, practices, disobedience, and departure from God by humanity. Has tribulation begun when the apple was eaten by the foreparents of this epoch ~ earth age or Adam and Eve? Is humanity presently continuing to be in it or be in the period of tribulation? The hardships, which comprise the tribulation, seemingly last through the opening of six out of seven seals; and the first seal is opened in Revelation 6:1. When the seventh seal is opened, in Revelation 8:1, it signals the start of God's wrath ~ anger, having been brought about by the sin of humanity during humanity's entire period of tribulation. The seventh seal is not opened until the end of the period of tribulation, Revelation 8:1. Revelation 8:1 is also the beginning of Elohim's wrath as a consequence of humanity's unrepentant acts of transgressions.

The period of tribulation, as has been stated previously, is sometimes referred to as wrath. Is this because it deals with hardships? However, these are hardships which were activated by humanity's own selfish desires to be disobedient to God—desire to be first. It is not Elohim's will; his desire for humanity to depart from him. God brought about a way for humanity's return to him. From day one, after humans fell, Elohim brought about a way, a plan to resurrect humanity unto himself. This he did through the virgin birth and resurrection of Jesus. Humanity, too, can be resurrected as Elohim's Son Jesus and experience only one death and a first resurrection as did Jesus. This is possible when one confesses Jesus to be the Son of Elohim and repents or admits being sorry or apologetic for one's sins. A reprobate, or a very bad person, or a dishonest person, does not turn away from sinful acts and is non-apologetic.

A reprobate person continues acts of sin. To be sorry is to repent. Repentance requires change or attempts to discontinue the sin. Change brings about freedom from repeating sin alongside realizing that repentance - change will bring about a first resurrection which is an escape from a second death—a second death consisting of fire and brimstone.

Division 1-B

The Tribulation Period: After the Condition of Religion

Revelation ca6:1-8:1

1-B. The Tribulation Period: After the Condition of Religion. Revelation ca6:1-ca8:1

Revelation 6

The Lamb opens the seals during the second part of the tribulation period. I call this period, the Tribulation Period: After the Condition of Religion, Revelation ca6:1-ca7:17. When the Lamb finishes opening his seals at the end of this tribulation period, Revelation 8:1, Revelation 8:1 also starts his wrath.

Revelation 6:1-2

Lamb opened seal one. One of the four beasts, whose voice sounded like thunder, tells John to come and see. John saw a white horse.

Revelation 6:3-4

Lamb opened seal two. The second beast said, "Come and see." John saw a red horse go out.

Revelation 6:5-6

Lamb opened seal three. The third beast said, "Come and see." John saw a black horse, and the horse held the world economy ~ a pair of balances in his hands. "The use of dishonest scales is the only unrighteous business practice that God calls an abomination," says Norm Franz, in his book, *Money and Wealth in the New Millennium*, p.11. Additionally, Proverbs 11:1 states the following about dishonest scales: "A false balance is an abomination to the Lord; but a just weight is his delight." Are false scales today being used to weigh the products brought about by a day's labor?

Seemingly, the economic system Elohim intended for His children is based on sharing or equal product distribution. Perhaps no one person should have total ownership of goods for self while others go wanting. Consider Acts 2:44-45 when it says, "And all that believed were together, and had all things common And sold their possessions and goods; and parted them to all men, as every man had need."

Surely, this is unlike the economic system which exists in today's global society. Remember how the rich man wanted to know how to be saved? Seemingly, after having kept all the commandments, he still felt empty. In Matthew 19:21, Jesus tells the man the following: "If thou wilt be perfect, go and sell that thou hast, and give to the poor, and thou shalt have treasure in heaven; and come and follow me."

Apparently, the man was putting his desire to have wealth ahead of his desire to have a relationship with Jesus.

Revelation 6:7-8	Lamb opened fourth seal. The fourth seal said, "Come and see." John saw a pale horse whose name was Death and Hell.
Revelation 6:9-11	When the Lamb opened the fifth seal, no beast spoke; but John saw souls under the altar who cried loudly, "How long, O Lord?" They were told to rest a little longer until time for their fellow servants had ended on earth and sea. How does Revelation 6:9-11 relate to Revelation 7:9-17? Are these the same souls who represent all the people who've lived and died on earth before, during, and after Jesus's life on earth?

Revelation 6:12-16   Lamb opened the sixth seal. There is a great earthquake.

Revelation 6:17   "For the great day of his wrath (anger) is come: and who shall be able to stand?"

Revelation 7:12   Four angels appeared. These four angles had been given authority to hurt the earth and seas. One angel appeared who held the seal of God.

Revelation 7:3   The angel who appeared holding the seal of God told the four angels, to whom it had been given authority to hurt the earth and sea, not to hurt the earth and sea until, "We have sealed the servants of God in their foreheads."

Revelation 7:4-8   John heard the number which were sealed. One hundred, forty-four thousand were sealed from all twelve tribes of Israel's sons:

- Tribe of Judah, twelve thousand
- Tribe of Reuben, twelve thousand
- Tribe of Gad, twelve thousand
- Tribe of Asher, twelve thousand
- Tribe of Nephthalim, twelve thousand
- Tribe of Manasses, twelve thousand
- Tribe of Simeon, twelve thousand
- Tribe of Levi, twelve thousand
- Tribe of Issachar, twelve thousand
- Tribe of Zabulon, twelve thousand
- Tribe of Joseph, twelve thousand
- Tribe of Benjamin, twelve thousand

Revelation 7:9-17   John saw a great multitude. Is Revelation 7:9-17 relative to Revelation 6:9-11? The people are so numerous until they cannot be counted. They come from every nation, kindred, people, and tongue. In Revelation 7:14, the elder asked, "Who are these people?" In Revelation 7:14, the elder is told, "You know, these are they which came out of the great tribulation." Can the 144,000 that John saw, which were sealed from all twelve tribes of Israel's sons, be part of the great multitude, out in Revelation 7:13; and who are in heaven before the tribulation period ends, and Elohim's wrath ~ anger begins? The end of the period of tribulation and the beginning of Elohim's wrath ~ anger seem to join at Revelation 8:10. Is this the millennium? How likely is it that the millennium exists within the tribulation periods and judgment? Consider that Jesus comes after judgment to establish his kingdom! These same 144,000 are seen again in Revelation 14:1. They are standing alongside the Lamb on Mount Zion, as the Lamb prepares to reap by thrusting in his sickle in Revelation 14:19. Concerning the "millennium," or the one thousand years the dragon is supposedly in "hell" according to the claims of the exhorters, could the millennium be as earth? Is earth as the bottomless pit to which the dragon is thrown from heaven into? Has the dragon existed on "earth" since he was thrown from heaven to earth, bringing accusations to Elohim about Elohim's creations? He died once by experiencing a departure from God when he was thrown from heaven. He did not fear Elohim. He lacked wisdom

207

and understanding. Will he be judged when the rest of the unrighteous will be judged and receive no resurrection but die a second time by being cast into a lake which burns with fire and brimstone forever after the battle between Gog and Magog? When an angel cries for the Lamb to thrust in his sickle, it signals a harvest is beginning or a harvest's beginning. Revelation 14:15 states, "And another angel came out of the temple, crying with a loud voice to him that sat on the clouds, thrust in thy sickle and reap: for the time has come for thee to reap: for the harvest of the earth is ripe."

Will the dragon's judgment occur after he is defeated at the Gog and Magog battle? A battle which seemingly takes place between good and evil. Is this battle after the battle of Armageddon? Gog and Magog are spoken about in Revelation 20:8 while Armageddon is spoken of in Revelation 16:16.

Regarding the multitude who are seen in Revelation 6:19-11, and again in Revelation 7:9-17, and who are asked about by one of the elders in Revelation 7:14, is it the same group of people or multitude who are with the Lamb?

Revelation 8	Seven angels with trumpets.
Revelation 8:2-5	Seven angels who stood before Elohim were given seven trumpets in preparation for the wrath of God. Another angel came before the altar who had a golden censor. The angel should

offer the incense, with the prayer of the saints, upon the altar which was before the throne.

Revelation 8:11   The Lamb opened the seventh seal. The opening of the seventh seal brings about the end of the tribulation periods and the beginning of the period ~ time ~ season of Elohim's wrath ~ anger, not judgment.

Division 2

Period of Wrath ~ Anger

Revelation ca8:1-ca14:18

2. Period of Wrath ~ Anger. Revelation ca8:1-ca14:18

The seven angels at the end of the seventh seal of tribulation, in Revelation 8:1, are the same seven angels of God's wrath which sounded their trumpets, signaling the start of Elohim's wrath, in Revelation 8:6. His anger continues until harvest starts at Revelation ca14:19.

Revelation 8:6   And the seven angels which had the seven trumpets prepared themselves to sound.

Revelation 8:8-7   The first angel sounded ~ blew his trumpets.

Revelation 8:8-9   The second angel sounded ~ blew his trumpet. A burning mountain fell into the sea and the sea became blood. Sea life and ships destroyed. War?

Revelation 8:10-11   The third angel sounded. A great star fell from heaven whose name was Wormwood. Wormwood made parts of the water bitter, and some parts of humanity died, or the water was poisoned.

Revelation 8:12   Fourth angel sounded. The third part of the sun, moon, and stars were smitten with darkness.

Revelation 8:13   One angel flies through heaven saying, in a loud voice, what woes the voices of the trumpets of the remaining three angels will bring about.

Revelation 9:1-12   The fifth angel sounded his trumpet. It brings about the first woe. A star fell from heaven and to him [that star] was given the key to the bottomless pit and large locusts came out.

The angel of the bottomless pit was king of the locusts. Revelation 20:2-3 says the dragon is restrained in a bottomless pit for a time, for one thousand years. Where in time should the millennium be placed?

Revelation 9:13-21   The sixth angel sounds, and brings about the second woe. The sixth angel is told to let loose the four angels which are bound to the river Euphrates. They were let loosed and prepared to slay one-third of the earth with all of the events brought forth by the loosening of these angels. Unfortunately, the men who remained alive on earth after this destruction still do not repent, according to Revelation 9:20-21.

Revelation 10:1-6   Before the voice of the seventh angel sounded, Jesus, the angel, came down from heaven and cried. When he cried, seven thunders uttered their voices. John was told not to write what the seven thunders' voices had said. Elohim will testify that, "There should be time no longer." Revelation 10:5 states, "And the angel which I saw stand upon the sea and upon the earth lifted up his hands to heaven. And swear by him that liveth forever and ever, who created heaven, and the things that therein are, and the earth, and the things that therein are, and the sea, and the things which are therein, that there should be time no longer."

Revelation 11   The seventh angel still has not yet sounded.

Revelation 11:1-2   John was told to measure the inside of the temple but not outside since the outside has been given to the Gentiles, and the holy city shall be treaded under foot for forty-two months, or three and a half years. Between what time should this forty-two months or three and a half years be sequenced?

Revelation 11: 3-12 Power given to two witnesses to give testimony about God. Eventually, they were killed. However, after three days, like Jesus, they were resurrected. An earthquake happens.

Revelation 11:15 The seventh angel sounds: "And the seventh angel sounded; and there were great voices, in heaven saying, the kingdom of this world are become the kingdoms of our Lord, and of his Christ, and he shall reign forever and ever.

Revelation 11:18 And the nations were angry, and thy wrath is come, and the time of the dead that they shall be judged. When is judgment? Judgment follows Elohim's wrath. Wrath and harvest appear to overlap, and judgment appears to escalate about Revelation 19:11. Will the enemy be released after the judgment of the unfaithful, the unbelieving in Revelation 19:11-20 to walk the earth again? His fate having already been sealed by receiving the second death in terms of being cast into the lake of fire in Revelation 20:10? Might this be as or be the millennium? If it is, will it occur after judgment, or has it already transpired?

Revelation 12:1-17 During Elohim's wrath, historical events appear. The virgin birth and the overthrow of the dragon or the enemy from heaven to make war with the woman and her child to earth is seen.

Revelation 13   John sees the beast. The enemy's imitation of the Trinity is as follows: the dragon is an imitation of Elohim, the beast is an imitation of Jesus, and the false prophet is an imitation of the Holy Spirit.

Revelation 14:1-5   To reiterate, it appears that the 144,000 miss God's wrath as a result of them being sealed during the tribulation in Revelation 7:3-8 and have been and are seen among and alongside the other sealed righteous at the end of the tribulation period which is before the wrath starts. The wrath starts at Revelation 8:1. Can this hypothesis be true, that because the 144,000 are seen again with the Lamb at the start of the harvest in Revelation 11:14, that they, alongside other followers of Jesus, have been in heaven since the end of tribulation and the start of the Lamb's harvest?

Revelation 14:6-17   John saw another angel fly into heaven who said, "Fear not ... for the hour of judgment (wrath) has come."

Revelation 14:8   Another angel followed crying, "Babylon is fallen."

Revelation 14:9-10   Another angel followed, warning, "Any man take the mark of the beast on his forehead or his hand, they shall drink of the wrath of God."

Division 3

Period of Harvest

Revelation ca14:19-ca19:10

3. Period of Harvest. Revelation ca14:19-ca19:10

The Lamb's sickle is thrust in at Revelation 14:19. This act signals that reaping has come. Can the premise that all the fruit ~ the righteous ~ the faithful ~ the sealed have been harvested since only the vines ~ the unrepentant ~ the unrighteous ~ the unfaithful ~ the unsealed ~ the unrepentant seem to remain to be harvested, to be validated? Notice that only the vines are gathered and are thrown into the winepress of the wrath of God. Is this the second judgment? Where have all the fruits gone? They seem to be missing. Did they experience the first resurrection? Revelation 14:19-20 states, "And the angel thrust in his sickle into the earth, and cast it into the great winepress of God. And the winepress was trodden without the city, and blood came out of the winepress, even unto the horse bridles. By the space of a thousand and six hundred furlongs."

Might this act signal a millennium's end or a millennium's approach?

Division 4

Judgment

Revelation ca19:11-21 and Revelation ca20:1-15

(The Lamb returns in Revelation 21, and the
Tree of Life is returned in Revelation 22)

Division 4. Judgment. Revelation ca19:11-21 and Revelation ca20:1-15

Judgment is foretold in the entire chapter of Revelation20, and the beast and the false prophet, the dragon's two helpers, are judged in Revelation 19:20 before Revelation 20. Revelation 19:20 states, "And the beast was taken, and with him the false prophet that wrought miracles before him, with which he deceived them that received the mark of the beast, and them that worshipped his image. These both were cast alive into a lake of fire burning with brimstone."

Is it highly likely that the dragon's home, since being cast from heaven, has been in a bottomless pit, and that bottomless pit could be earth? Revelation 20:2-3 speaks of this bottomless pit. How likely is it that the earth is as a bottomless pit? The dragon's temporary dwelling until he is sent to his eternal place of dwelling or the lake of fire burning with brimstone.

How likely is it that the dragon and his two helpers, the beast and the false prophet, have not one but two deaths, the physical and the spiritual, since they are as the unfaithful? How likely is it that the faithful experience the first resurrection, and the unfaithful experience two resurrections, one unto the grave and one unto the their final destination of fire burning with brimstone, or the first and second deaths? Revelation 20:5-6 speaks of the first resurrection and the second death. It states, "But the rest of the dead lived not again until the thousand years were finished. This is the first resurrection. Blessed and holy is he that hath part in the first resurrection on such the second death hath no power, but they shall be priests of God and of Christ."

Synopsis

A Compilation of the
Divisions of Revelation

Revelation 1-22

An Interpretative Focus
An exhorted, interpretative focus alongside a revealed focus.
Nothing has been added nor taken away (Revelation 22:18-19).

Synopsis

Prior to approximately Revelation 5, John sees the condition of religion, and he sees the throne. This condition has been coined "Division 1-A, the Tribulation Period: the Condition of Religion, Revelation 1:1-5:13." In Revelation 5:4-7, the Lamb is found worthy to be the one to open and read the book and to let loose the seven seals when it is time for them to be loosed. In Revelation 6:9, which is part of the Tribulation Period: After the Condition of Religion, souls are seen. Revelation 6:9 states, "When the Lamb opened the fifth seal, I saw under the altar the souls of them that were slain for the Word of God, and for the testimony they held."

Who are these souls who are out from the earth before the Lamb's Second Coming? Out from the grave?

Are these the souls who were out before Jesus's first coming? Souls who went out during his life on earth, and souls who have gone out since his life on earth ended, only to eventually be returning with him for a second time? The Lamb opened the sixth seal in Revelation 6:12. Revelation 6:12 belongs to Division B, the Tribulation Period: After the Condition of Religion, Revelation ca.6:1-7:17. After its opening in Revelation 6:12, in Revelation 7:2-8 the four angels, to whom it was given authority to hurt the earth and sea, were warned not to hurt the earth and sea until the servants of God were sealed. The number sealed is 144,000. Is to be sealed as to believe or to confess that Jesus is the Son of God? Hence, should the 144,000 who are sealed in Revelation 7:3-9 be included in the multitude who do stand before the throne in heaven in Revelation 7:9-17 even before Elohim starts his season of anger ~ wrath in Revelation 8:1? Some exhorters hypothesize about the occurrence of a rapture. Might this Jewish migration to heaven be as a rapture? A rapture of all Jews and non-Jews who have been sealed or believed that Jesus Christ is the only begotten, Divine Son of Elohim and the Savior of humanity?

When the seventh seal is opened in Revelation 8:1, the last of tribulation or the section labeled, Division 1-B, the Tribulation Period: After the Condition of Religion, Revelation ca.6:1-ca.8:1, would have occurred; and it opens Elohim's wrath ~ anger from Revelation 8:1-14:18. Therefore, it can be considered that Revelation 14:19 starts Elohim's reaping since this is the time when the Lamb thrusts in his sickle to harvest to gather, to clear the earth of its vines. Are the vines the garden's debris? Where is the fruit? Prior to the time of reaping, past, current, and future time appear, events are shown. Time and events involving the dragon's relationship with the Baby Jesus and humanity. Obvious in the scene is that before time, there must have been in heaven two powerful agents—one agent having created the second agent. The second agent, dissatisfied with a lower status, rebelled against the first agent—his authority, Elohim.

Is there conflict in heaven? Is there war in heaven? Is this conflict synonymous with earth's Gog and Magog? Does it close one millennium in order to bring about another millennium? Does it close one millennium and open a new millennium? Is this destiny? Is it Elohim's destiny? Is it Elohim's purpose? Is it what Elohim desires? Is it God's plan? Is it God's plan to close one millennium and open another millennium, a new millennium, a new millennium in heaven alongside on earth? A new Adam and Eve? Possibly, new types of creatures? This new kingdom ~ this dry earth will be refreshed with new water! Every creature, beast and man, shall be refreshed with new water. Everyone shall be given the opportunity to make right choices amid circumstances. Elohim commands that the earth's creatures, human and nonhuman, obey his Word, his voice. God created things to be obedient. He obviously has faith that man will be obedient and respectful. To pledge one's allegiance to another thing or things opposite God is disrespectful to God and does lead to departure from Elohim. Nothing will be allowed to disrespect ~ disrupt God's order. He will bring about new millenniums, establish new earths with his intervention.

In the vision involving the dragon's relationship with Mary and her Son Jesus, Mary is shown having conceived her baby and her attempts to protect her child. Revelation 12:1-2, 12:5, 12:6, and 12:14-17 reveal Mary and her baby. Is this Israel?

And there appeared a great wonder in heaven; a woman clothed with the sun, and the moon under her feet, and upon her head a crown of twelve stars: (v.1)

And she being with child cried, travailing in birth, and pained to be delivered (v.2).

And she brought forth a man child, who was to rule all nations with a rod of iron: and her child was caught up unto God, and to his throne (v.5).

And the woman fled into the wilderness, where she hath a place prepared of God, that they should feed her there a thousand two hundred and threescore days (v.6).

And to the woman were given two wings of a great eagle, that she might fly into the wilderness, into her place, where she is nourished for a time, and times, and half a time, from the face of the serpent (v.14).

And the serpent cast out of his mouth water as a flood after the woman, that he might cause her to be carried away from the flood (v.15).

And the earth helped the woman, and the earth opened her mouth, and swallowed up the flood which the dragon cast out of his mouth (v.16).

And the dragon was wroth with the woman, and went to make war with the remnant of her seed, which keep the commandments of God, and have the testimony of Jesus Christ (v.17).

The dragon is shown alongside Mary the Virgin in Revelation 12:3-4 and 12:7-13. Those verses state:

And there appeared another wonder in heaven; and behold a great red dragon, having seven heads and ten horns, and seven crowns upon his heads (v.3).

And his tail drew the third part of the stars of heaven, and did cast them to earth: and the dragon stood before the woman which was ready to be delivered, for to devour her child as soon as it was born (v.4).

And there was war in heaven: Michael and his angels fought against the dragon; and the dragon fought and his angels (v.7).

And prevailed not; neither was their place found any more in heaven (v.8).

And the great dragon was cast out, that old serpent, called the Devil, and Satan, which deceiveth the whole world: he was cast out into the earth, and his angels were cast out with him (v.9).

And I heard a loud voice saying in heaven, Now is come salvation, and strength, and the kingdom of our God, and the power of his Christ: for the accuser of our brethren is cast down, which accused them before our God day and night (v.10).

And they overcame him by the blood of the Lamb, and by the word of their testimony; and they loved not their lives unto the death (v.11).

Therefore rejoice, ye heavens, and ye that dwell in them. Woe to the inhabiters of the earth and of the sea! for the devil is come down unto you, having great wrath, because he knoweth that he hath but a short time (v.12).

And when the dragon saw that he was cast unto the earth, he persecuted the woman which brought forth the man child (v.13).

Armageddon is a battle, and it occurs before God and Magog—a world battle between good and evil which apparently brings about the defeat of Babylon. It occurs in Revelation 16:16. What or who is Babylon? America? Is America a land that sits on many waters, as does Babylon? Revelation 17:1 states, "And there came one of the seven angels which had the seven vials, and talked with me, saying unto me, Come hither: I will show unto thee the judgment of the great whore that sitteth upon many waters."

Several years ago, I asked Elohim, "Where is America in the Bible? He answered, "America is the land that sits on many waters." This answer correlates with Revelation 17:1. Might this answer include other nations?

Judgment appears to begin at Revelation ca.19:11. It extends through the entire chapter of Revelation 20. The dragon and other unrighteous need to be judged. Some of the unrighteous have died and are waiting on judgment, or their second death. The righteous appear to be judged at death and go directly to heaven with no second death. The books are opened. I hypothesize that these plural books signal that it is time for the unrighteous to be "tied" bound ~ yoked ~ judged, both the one's out of the grave or who are physically alive, alongside the ones who are in the grave and are physically dead.

Revelation 20:12 states, "And I saw the dead, small and great, stand before God; and the books were opened: and another book was opened, which is the book of life: and the dead were judged out of those things which were written in the books, according to their works."

Is there a book of life for the unrighteous alongside a book of life for the righteous?

Life after death? According to the *Dictionary of the Bible*, edited by James Hastings, inequality of this life made the lack of a doctrine of future rewards a theological problem with which men increasingly wrestled. There were those who were confident that Yahweh rules also in Sheol, or hell, and would vindicate them there or set them free from blame ~ guilt. Sheol, or hell, as the abode of the dead pending judgment is "wrestled" with by today's Christianity alongside the resurrection of Jesus Christ. His body did not see corruption in Hades. Acts 2:31 states, "He seeing this before spake of the resurrection of Christ, that his soul was not left in hell, neither his flesh did see corruption."

Jesus has the keys of death and Hades. Revelation 1:18 says, "I am he that liveth, and was dead, and, behold, I am alive for evermore, Amen: and have the keys of hell and of death."

The notion of Sheol (the grave?) as the abode of the dead pending judgment continued with some Jews but was abandoned by others. Belief in resurrection established itself among Jews; although even in New Testament times, the Sadducees rejected it. The Sadducee's belief was that Sheol ~ grave is divided into compartments for the righteous who have gone unpunished on the earth and for sinners who have suffered somewhat. That Sheol, the grave, holds all the dead until judgment remains as a belief by some present-day followers of Jesus or Christians.

Between Revelation 15:11 (inside the harvest) and Revelation 19:11(the last of Judgment) these are things which occur:

Revelation 15:1	Plagues
Revelation 15:2	Some men have gotten the victory over the beast and over his image and mark.
Revelation 16:2	There fell a noisome and grievous sore upon the men which had the mark of the beasts and upon them which worshipped his image.
Revelation 16:3	The sea became as the blood of a dead man, and every living soul died in the sea.
Revelation 16:9	Men were scorched with great heat and blasphemed the name God, which hath power over these plagues; and they did not repent to give him glory.
Revelation 16:10	The fifth angel poured out his vial upon the seat or the home of the beast, which is the same as earth. The earth became dark, yet man did not repent and give glory and honor to God.
Revelation 16:11	Men called God profane names or names which showed disrespect and lack of honor of God.
Revelation 16:12	Waters dried up in the river Euphrates.
Revelation 16:14	The spirits of devils worked miracles.
Revelation 16:16	He gathered them together into a place called in the Hebrew tongue, Armageddon.
Revelation 16:18	There was a great earthquake.
Revelation 16:19	The cities of the nations fell, bringing Babylon in the remembrance of God and

	the need to give her the fierceness of his wrath.
Revelation 16:20	Every island fled away until the mountains could not be found.
Revelation 16:21.	Hail, the size of a talent, fell upon men which caused men to blaspheme God.
Revelation 17:1	The judgment of the great whore who sits on many waters is seen.
Revelation17:9	The woman sits on seven mountains.
Revelation 17:10-11	Each of the seven mountains is ruled by a different king, and the eight is ruled by the beast.
Revelation 17:13	Each king has a mind to give their power and strength to the beast.
Revelation 18:2-3	Babylon is fallen because all nations have drunk of the wrath of her fornication. The merchants of the nations have been made rich by her waves.
Revelation 18:8	The consequence of Babylon's fornication is that her plagues will cause in one day death, famine, and mourning; she shall be utterly destroyed by fire.
Revelation 18:11-19	The merchants will weep at the loss of capitalism or their inability to capitalize off of buying and selling, thereby depriving them of their ability to accumulate wealth and riches.
Revelation 18:22-24	No more music will reside in her, nor electricity, and no woman being given in marriage to the male. The blood of the prophets will be Babylon's responsibility.
Revelation 19:7	Be glad and rejoice because the marriage of the Lamb is about to come ~ to be brought about.

Revelation 14:9   Blessed are those who are called to the Lamb's wedding supper.

A new kingdom is shown in Revelation 2:1, with the Lamb as the healer of all nations. This healing is subsequently symbolized by the return of the tree of life. Revelation 22:1-2 states, "And he showed me a pure river of water of life, clear as crystal, proceeding out of the throne of God and of the Lamb. In the midst of the street of it, and on either side of the river, was there the tree of life, which bare twelve manner of fruits, and yielded her fruit every month: and the leaves of the tree were for the healing of the nations."

Before the appearance of the new kingdom, John sees the preparations the Lamb makes for his bride alongside his judgment of the unjust (Rev. 19:1-21 and Rev. 20:1-15). In Revelation 22, we see the tree of life returned to the garden—Africa/Eden, Africa, Middle East? Europe? Its return symbolizes that there is no more suffering, no more sin alongside the reign of the Jewish Messiah—Jesus? Is this a new millennium? Another millennium?

ABOUT THE AUTHOR

Beverly Fontenot spent most of her adult years teaching art and various other academics in the Denver public schools. Prior to teaching, she received her bachelor's degree in art history in addition to drawing and painting from Kansas University. She first pursued her training in education from Loretto Heights College (Denver, Colorado). Later, she continued at Colorado University alongside Denver University. She earned a master's degree in education and attended lliff School of Theology. At lliff School of Theology, she studied Christian Education. As a Christian, she's always been interested in understanding the Bible. She uses a nontraditional approach when she studies the Bible. She uses the New Testament to fit into the Old Testament or the Old Testament to fit into the New Testament. She feels the Scriptures are as parts. They should be fitted together as a puzzle. Consequently, she fits both parts together as a whole. She mostly does not sequence books.